Embracing The

"Looking for a theologically profound book that is easy to comprehend and can guide you towards a closer relationship with your Maker? If that is you, then *The Greatest Presence of All* is a must read! Through his comprehensive study of the names of God, Jim Herring has revealed a means of forging a deeper connection with our Creator. Jim's wisdom as a pastor and teacher shines through as he presents biblical concepts in a relatable manner for contemporary readers. The passion that Jim holds for God is palpable in every chapter."

Jaylene Stark, LMHC Licensed Mental Health Clinician, Bethel Ridge Family Resources

"In a world overflowing with books about God that are great but often technical, theological, and sometimes boring, Jim Herring's *Greatest Presence of All* stands out in the crowd for being strongly orthodox yet simple and accessible. Jim's writing style is easy, smooth, and conversational, making you feel like you are talking with him at a coffee shop. As you read, not only does Jim teach you about who God is through the names given to God in Scripture, but he leads you to experience the power of the presence of God in your own life. Whether you describe yourself as a Christian or not, Jim's book is a gift to you, leading you to a deeper intimacy with God and His love for you."

Kevin Deyette, Pastor, Restoration Church

"Jim uses this study of the various names of God found in the pages of Scripture to paint a clear picture of who God is and His plan of redemption for us, fulfilled in the person of Jesus Christ. This book provides a fantastic introduction to God as He reveals Himself throughout the story of the Bible for someone beginning their journey of faith. It also serves to, in Jim's own words, "reassure those who are already redeemed…that they possess an eternal, unbreakable relationship with their Creator.""

Dan Brown, Executive Director, Love INC

"Jim's weaving of personal story and testimony are effective at helping the reader understand the otherwise challenging aspects of understanding God's character and nature."

Todd Lundberg, Superintendent, Riverside Christian School

The Greatest Presence *of* All

God's Gift of Intimacy

Jim Herring

© 2023 by James Herring

All rights reserved worldwide. No part of this book may be used or reproduced in any manner whatsoever without written permission, except in the case of brief quotations in critical articles and reviews.

Print ISBN: 979-8-35092-797-9
eBook ISBN: 979-8-35092-798-6

Editing by Linda Nathan, Logos Word Designs, LLC

Published by BookBaby Publishing

Unless otherwise indicated, Scripture quotations taken from the Holy Bible, New International Version® NIV®, Copyright © 1973, 1978, 1984, 2011by Biblica, Inc. ® Used by permission. All rights reserved worldwide.

Scripture marked New American Standard Version taken from the (NASB®) New American Standard Bible®, Copyright © 1960, 1962, 1963, 1968, 1971, 1972, 1973, 1975, 1977, 1995, 2020 by The Lockman Foundation. Used by permission. All rights reserved. Lockman.org

Scripture marked New King James Version taken from the New King James Version, Copyright © 1979, 1980, 1982 by Thomas Nelson, Inc. Used by permission, All rights reserved.

To my precious wife: my love, friend, counsellor, and advocate.

She has taught me what intimacy and constant companionship are all about.

CONTENTS

INTRODUCTION 1

CHAPTER 1: A TALE OF TWO STORIES 3

CHAPTER 2: REFLECTIONS OF MAJESTY(Elohim)................13

CHAPTER 3: A SPECIAL MOMENT(Yahweh) 18

CHAPTER 4: MAKING WAR ON THE FLOOR(El Elyon).................... 23

CHAPTER 5: WHAT A DIFFERENCE A NAME MAKES
(El Roi and El Shaddai) 29

CHAPTER 6: FROM HERE TO ETERNITY(EL OLAM) 35

CHAPTER 7: WHAT A PLACE! WHAT A NAME!(Yahweh Yireh) 39

CHAPTER 8: INTO THE WILDERNESS
(Yahweh Rapha, Yahweh Nissi, Yahweh M' Kaddesh).................... 44

CHAPTER 9: OF TEETER-TOTTERS AND CYCLES(Yahweh Shalom) 52

CHAPTER 10: WHO'S IN YOUR FOX HOLE?(Yahweh Sabaoth).................... 58

CHAPTER 11: THAT'S RIGHT!(Yahweh Tsidkenu)................................63

CHAPTER 12: AND THE NAME OF THE CITY IS....
(Yahweh Shammah).. 67

CHAPTER 13: IMMANUEL'S LAND(Immanuel)..71

CHAPTER 14: TWO SIDES OF ONE COIN(Savior/Jesus and Lord) 76

CHAPTER 15 : IRON MAN WITH A KIPPAH (Messiah) 82

CHAPTER 16: I WOULD LIKE TO SPEAK WITH
        THE PERSON IN CHARGE(God) 89

CHAPTER 17: PAID IN FULL AND ON TIME!(Redeemer)................................96

CHAPTER 18: "IT'S JESUS...IT'S IN HIM!"(Alpha and Omega) 101

CHAPTER 19: A TALE OF TWO PRAYERS...104

APPENDIX A: QUIZ ANSWERS..109

APPENDIX B: WHY YAHWEH?..111

APPENDIX C: A WORD ON ANTINOMIES...112

ACKNOWLEDGMENTS...115

INTRODUCTION

CENTURIES BEFORE THE covid pandemic, loneliness had perfected the art of social isolation. People all over the world have experienced the absence of intimacy, even among close companions. It is a universal scourge that has robbed millions of the joy of experiencing a deep, abiding relationship. Try as one might, loneliness sticks to the soul like Velcro. Attempts to eradicate this emotional tyrant end in even deeper feelings of isolation.

This book takes a realistic look at loneliness and how we can gain the high ground in our struggle to be free from this menace. By looking at this problem through the lens of Scripture, the reader can begin to see that intimacy, properly grounded in a deep abiding relationship with our Creator, provides the emotional and intellectual strength and support needed to push back against this insidious enemy.

Several chapters are devoted to an explanation of some of the names and titles of God. This approach, however, isn't simply an academic endeavor. Instead, the strategy is to compare these names and titles in the historical context in which they were revealed. By doing so, a surprising reality emerges: God makes himself known to us precisely at the junction of human experience. Intimacy ensues when divine revelation and human needs connect. Scripture reveals that God is present with us in a multitude of circumstances. He's with us in creation, as we enter the promised land, journey into the wilderness, or come into captivity. He heals, empowers, restores, provides, sustains, and gives victory to His followers.

The Bible reaches its grand finale in the person of Jesus Christ, God's only begotten Son. It is in him that the fullest light of divine intimacy shines unabated. In Christ, the human heart finds peace, fulfillment, and release from the pangs of loneliness.

To preserve the harmony and flow of the text, some technical information occurs in the appendices at the end of the book and in the footnotes.

CHAPTER 1
A TALE OF TWO STORIES

YOUR NEIGHBOR HAS three chickens. Someone just won ten million dollars. You just won ten million dollars. Suppose each statement is true. Which one matters the most to you? I may be going out on a limb here, but my guess is everyone would choose the third statement. Unless the chickens came to your yard and laid golden eggs, who cares how many chickens your neighbor has? It's nice that someone now has ten million dollars, but again, unless they choose to share some of their winnings with you, it does nothing to make a difference in your life. But the fact that **you** won ten million dollars, well, that's a different story.

What would you do if you received so much money? Maybe you'd buy a house or a car, perhaps both. You may want to travel to an exotic country like Egypt, France, India, or Montana (sorry, Montana is not a country). No, quit your job and move to an exotic country. How about buying an RV and heading out on Route 66? Whatever you do, chances are things in your life will be different, at least as long as the money lasts.

The two stories that follow show that God's presence makes a difference in our lives. The first is my testimony of how entering into a personal relationship with God through his Son Jesus Christ was life-transforming. The second shows that what happened in my life has happened to millions of others as well.

Subjective feelings and personal needs are important, but these are not the catalyst for change. Instead, the reality of God's existence and his desire to enter a personal relationship with us all has been and continues to be the common life-transforming experience of people for thousands of years.

MY STORY

I met my wife in the gutter. By this, I don't mean a chance encounter in a back alley in east L.A. Instead, I met her at the Wonder Bowl in Anaheim, California, located right next to Disneyland. As a Marine back in 1968 stationed at Santa Ana Helicopter Airbase, I happened to join a bowling team. I was a lousy bowler, but it was something to do to break the incessant boredom of staying in the barracks.

On the fourth trip to Wonder Bowl, I glanced over about five lanes and saw a young woman ready to bowl. Her long hair and graceful poise caught my attention…and my heart. I thought how great it would be to get to know her, but five lanes away might as well have been the end of the world. Why would she want to know someone like me? I was just one of many Jarheads on liberty trying to find something to fill the time.

To my surprise, when she and her friend finished bowling, they came over and sat in a booth right behind us. I was both excited and terrified, eager to meet her and afraid she might rebuff any attempts to get to know her. Finally, I mustered up the courage and went back to speak to her. I managed to say something profound…"Hi."

I almost struck out, but God spared me (bowling puns intended). Rather than tell me to get lost, she graciously continued the conversation that in short order developed into a deepened relationship. I could hardly wait for liberty to spend time with her. We'd travel to the beach, catch a movie, or spend hours at her house playing board games with her mother and stepfather.

Sometimes when I called her on the phone, she'd ask what I wanted to do when we got together. I often told her it didn't matter what we did as long as we were together. I know that sounds sappy, but it brings to the surface an important point—we are designed to thrive in an abiding relationship with the one we love and cherish.

Toward the end of 1968, I received West Pac orders. I was going to Vietnam. Ironically, I believed I was prepared to fight and kill if necessary, but I wasn't prepared to die. The Marine Corps had diligently disciplined me to carry out the former but neglected to deal effectively with the consequences of the latter.

As I wrestled with this dilemma, we were invited to a Billy Graham Crusade at the Anaheim baseball stadium. We got there late and had to sit on the bleachers all the way at the end of the first base line. They had set up a platform near the pitcher's mound, and Billy Graham spoke to the crowd with his back to us.

He talked about a God who desires to have fellowship with us. I'd always believed a supernatural being existed, but I'd never considered that a personal relationship with God was possible or even what that would mean in my life. He continued to convey the truth that because we've sinned, a deep chasm now exists between God and ourselves. However, the good news was that Jesus, His only begotten Son, came to this earth as a man and died on the cross to pay the penalty for our sins. If we confessed that Jesus died and rose again, our sins would be forgiven, and we could enter an abiding relationship with God.

The most striking point Billy Graham made was that this new relationship could never be broken. No matter what happens to us, we can have the assurance that God will always be with us. This truth pierced my heart. I knew that having the assurance of an eternal relationship with God was the very thing missing in my life.

As the crusade drew to a close, Billy Graham extended an invitation that anyone who desired to put their faith in Jesus could come down and stand in front of the platform and pray for this wonderful gift of salvation. Many people throughout the stadium got up and went forward. I, too, had a deep desire, but for some reason, I stayed back. I wanted to know that this was God's will for my life.

I cried out to God to give me a sign that He was the one leading me to His Son. At that very moment, Billy Graham stopped talking. He turned around toward us and, pointing his finger in our direction said, "Jim, come down here right now." Then he turned around and continued speaking. This was just what I needed. I'm sure there were many "Jims" in the bleachers, but one was wearing my shirt and had received an answer to his prayer. With all reservations swept away, I immediately arose and went forward with my fiancé to put our trust in Jesus.

Shortly thereafter, I left for Vietnam. I was assigned to HML-167, a helicopter gunship squadron at Marble Mountain Helicopter Airbase just outside of Da Nang. Once settled in, I looked up the base chaplain. I told him I'd just put my trust in Christ for my salvation and was eager to learn more about the person who would love me enough to sacrifice himself on my behalf.

He met my plea for discipling with outright rejection and told me if I wanted to be discipled, I could come to his Sunday services along with everyone else. He made it clear he had no time (or desire) to meet one-on-one with me.

It's possible I didn't understand the demands and expectations placed on a chaplain in a war zone, but I left deeply discouraged and determined I'd never attend any of his services. I kept my promise, but unfortunately, by doing so, I cut myself off from contact with other Marines who may have shared my convictions and desires.

It wasn't long before I became acquainted with violence and death. While on the ground, I was assigned to maintenance control; but when flying, I was a machine gunner providing air support for recon insurgents and medivac missions. Once, I even flew as a decoy along the "rocket belt."

As the months passed, I gradually gave up hope of ever returning home. I became fatalistic, thinking the inevitable was bound to happen no matter what I did. As a result, I stopped taking care of myself. I no longer sent my clothes for cleaning or changed the linens on my rack (cot). Whenever I flew, I'd toss the lead-lined bullet bouncer meant to protect my chest onto the helicopter floor.

With the fear of death emerged a sinister twin—loneliness. I began to feel isolated, cut off from everyone who knew and cared about me. Because I had no contact with any other Christians, the intense desire I once had to know God more grew cold. The very idea of a loving and caring God in the crucible of war seemed unreal and distant.

A day came when I returned to my hooch (the hut where we lived) from another medivac mission. It was late in the evening, and I'd missed chow (dinner) again. My flight suit was soaked from exposure to the monsoon rain. As I stood in my small cubicle, I looked down at the rack where I slept. I could see the outline of my body stained on the sheet. Suddenly it dawned on me that this is what I had become, a dirty stain in this hellhole of a place. A deep sense of emptiness enveloped me. My thoughts were freefalling into a fathomless sea of nothingness. I was drowning in despair, and there was no one there to save me.

I was about to say to myself that I was completely alone when suddenly a warm feeling swept over me. It was as though I'd stuck my finger in an outlet: my whole being tingled with an unfamiliar yet peaceful sensation. Unexpectedly, I realized I wasn't alone. God had, in fact, travelled with me to this place. He hadn't forsaken me after all. He was with me!

The reality of His presence was transformative. My hopelessness quickly dissipated. Even though I continued to fly, I began to allow myself to think I could possibly survive. The crushing fear of death and loneliness gave way to the prospect of returning home. I began to live again.

The desire for discipling when I first came to Vietnam resurfaced. Although I continued to boycott chapel services, I came to believe the God present in my life would also guide me to a source wherein I could get to know him more.

I told another sergeant there was a library located somewhere on the base, and I was convinced it held a book that would tell me more about Christ. Unfortunately, I had no clue where it was. We set out walking between row after row of hooches and buildings hoping to find this hidden treasure. Finally, we came upon a Quonset hut with a small sign nailed to the metal siding next to the door: "Library." We'd arrived.

Bookshelves lined the walls. In the middle of the hut was a table, and on it was a single book. I picked it up and read the title: *The Life of Christ* by R. L. Bruckberger. I turned to my partner and said, "This is it." How odd. It took almost an hour to find the library and less than two minutes to discover the book. Since I still have it, it may be the most overdue book on the planet!

I set to work reading page after page dedicated to the Person of Christ. What happened was more than I expected. Not only was I fed, but I discovered that I wanted to serve the Lord who sacrificed himself for me. Just before I left for home, I got down on my knees and committed my life to Jesus. I remember saying that I had no idea how he could possibly use someone like me, but I gave him my life to be used to His glory.

It's been fifty-two years since I said that prayer. My wife and I have three sons, a daughter, and ten grandchildren. I went to school and received a bachelor's degree and two master's degrees. Upon graduation, we spent some time on staff with Campus Crusade for Christ (now called Cru). We then transitioned into the church where I served as Director of Christian Education and Youth Pastor for four years. I was ordained as a minister in the Conservative Baptist Association. From there, I was a pastor for ten years. As of this writing, I've been a high school Bible teacher for the past thirty years.

My wife and I have received the opportunity to take a youth group into central Mexico. We've stood atop the Pyramid of the Sun at Teotihuacan and seen Mexican farmers pray to receive Christ at the conclusion of our evening services. We've prayed for Muslims as we travelled from Istanbul and several cities ending at Ankara. We led students five years in a row to a village called Terra Blanche in Haiti. There, we came to tears listening to over 400 Haitian children singing praises to the Lord under a gigantic mango tree.

Since Vietnam, the Lord has allowed us some wonderful experiences, but life can also take you through deep valleys as well. Still, in all these years, I've never sensed that God was not present in my life. I've come to believe that the prospect of the absence of God is the most debilitating and destructive state a person can experience. It would be hell.

THE LORD'S STORY

While some people may identify with my story, especially Vietnam veterans, it lacks the authoritative and objective power necessary to convince others that God is personal and that he in any way seeks to be with us. After all, if he's the Creator of this vast universe, why would he desire to or even care about such lowly creatures as us. The late Carl Sagan once made this comment about the photo of the earth sent by *Voyager I* about 4 billion miles away: "Our planet is a lonely speck in the great enveloping cosmic dark. In our obscurity, in all this vastness, there is no hint that help will come from elsewhere to save us from ourselves."[1]

Ironically, God seemed to anticipate such feelings of insignificance amid his vast creation. The Psalmist wondered long ago, "When I consider your heavens, the work of your fingers, the moon and the stars, which you have

---

[1]   Carl Sagan, *Pale Blue Dot A Vision of the Human Future in Space* (New York: Random House, 1994), p. 9. To counter Carl Sagan's thesis, I recommend the teleological evidence presented by Guillermo Gonzalez and Jay W. Richards in their book, *The Privileged Planet.*

set in place, what is mankind that you are mindful of them, human beings that you care for them?" (Psalm 8:3–4).

At the time this psalm was written, the observable universe was limited to the keen eyes of a Palestinian shepherd as he gazed in wonder at the stars above him. Today, with the aid of powerful telescopes and the Hubble satellite, we can investigate deep space. What appeared as pale blue dots from the earth often turned out to be whole galaxies each containing over a 100 billion stars. Oddly enough, such discoveries both expand our thinking of the universe and shrink our feelings of significance even further. It's no wonder humans feel isolated and alone.

Fortunately, God has not left us to ponder the essence of our existence through the lens of our own thinking. He's chosen to reveal himself in ways that have the potential to collapse the distance between us and him. And he's done this in the most intimate and caring way.

Amazingly, the closer we come to our Creator, the more we become like His Son (see Romans 8:29; 2 Corinthians 3:18).

One way God has done this is by using names and titles. There may be many reasons why our parents gave us the names we now enjoy (or are condemned to live with). They may have given you a first or a middle name like one of your kinfolks. Maybe they just like the sound of the name. Perhaps in desperation they got a book of names, closed their eyes, turned to a page and pointed to a name…"Randy M"… Lucky you!

It may be a stretch, but some parents have given their children personal identifiers based upon the meaning of the names they chose. Even more, they've hoped that one day their child's character would correspond to their given name. "David" means "beloved," "Joseph" means "May Jehovah add or increase," and "Grace" means "charm, goodness and generosity." My first name is "James." It means "supplanter or substitute." *What?*

God has chosen many names by which to reveal himself. Each name's meaning reveals a certain aspect of his character. As a result, we can get to know God based on these many personal designations.

But wait! There's still more. Our Lord has done something profound. He's chosen to reveal his names in a manner corresponding to the lived experiences of his people. The names of God weren't randomly placed in the Bible but rather carefully chosen by God Himself so we can see that He's involved in our lives in ways that make a difference. His story is interwoven with our stories in such a way as to produce a grand tale of intimate proportions.

Before we get into the many names and titles of God in the following chapters, let's see how much you already know by taking this brief quiz. Try to match the names and titles of God with their respective meanings. You can check how well you did with the answers in Appendix A at the end of the book.

Warning: No Cheating! Bad things may happen…just saying!

Names and Titles of God Quiz

____Most High – Mighty/Mighty One

A. Elohim

____The Self-existent One

B. Adonai

____Yahweh is My Banner

C. El Shaddai

____Yahweh Who Heals

D. Yahweh Shalom

____God

E. Soter

____Mighty One – Majestic

F. Yahweh Rapha

____Yahweh Our Righteousness

G. Alpha & Omega

____Lord & Master

H. Yahweh

THE GREATEST PRESENCE OF ALL

____Savior

____Almighty God/All-sufficient

____Yahweh Will Provide

____Yahweh is Peace

____Jesus – Yahweh is Savior

____Messiah – The Anointed One

____Yahweh of Hosts/Armies

____The God Who Sees Me

____The Everlasting God

____The Lord Sanctifies, Makes Me Holy

____The Lord is Present

____Beginning & The End

I. Theos/El

J. El Elyon

K. Yahweh Nissi

L. Yahweh Sabbaoth

M. Christos

N. Yahweh Tsidkenu

O. Yahweh Yireh

P. Yahweh M'Kaddesh

Q. Yahweh Shammah

R. El Roi

S. El Olam

T. Yeshua/Iesous

CHAPTER 2

REFLECTIONS OF MAJESTY

(Elohim)

IN THE FIRST verse of the Bible, we encounter "God." Wait. That's getting ahead of ourselves. The word "God" is an English word. The Bible wasn't translated into English until 1380 A.D. by John Wycliffe. Depending on one's bibliographical calculus, the original text of Scripture was written in Hebrew many centuries earlier. Thus, if you were reading the Hebrew Bible (*Tanakh*), Genesis 1:1 would say "Elohim" created the heavens and the earth.

The word "Elohim" means at the very least "Mighty One"—referring to His power and majesty. The choice of this name fits perfectly within the context of creation. If the universe is the effect of a personal cause, that cause must be of immense power and might.

Elohim is both a sufficient and necessary appellation for the one who formed the stars. He established an earthly platform upon which a vast array of flora and fauna could flourish. Elohim determined the order upon which the natural world operates. The universe has been finely tuned to bring forth intelligent life in the same way the strings of a violin have been tightened to produce beautiful music. The whole universe sings in praise to "Elohim."

Not only does his name speak of infinite power, it also speaks of his majesty. He has the right to rule over what he has created. As Elohim, he exercises dominion over everything in heaven and earth because everything owes its very existence to his creative intentions.

The Psalmist extolled the majesty of God: "Lord, our Lord, how majestic is your name in all the earth! You have set your glory in the heavens" {Psalm 8:1). Nothing less than praises ascribing glory to his name is a fitting response from his creation:

> Ascribe to the LORD the glory due his name; worship
> the LORD in the splendor of his holiness. The voice
> of the LORD is over the waters; the God (Elohim)
> of glory thunders, the LORD thunders over the
> mighty waters. The voice of the LORD is powerful;
> the voice of the LORD is majestic (Psalm 29:2–4).

Amid all his creation, Elohim made someone special. He made our first parents. The Genesis account of creation continues:

> Then God (Elohim) said, "Let us make mankind in our
> image, in our likeness, so that they may rule over the fish
> in the sea and the birds in the sky, over the livestock and
> all the wild animals, and over all the creatures that move
> along the ground." So, God (Elohim) created mankind in
> his own image, in the image of God (Elohim) he created
> them; male and female he created them. God (Elohim)
> blessed them and said to them, "Be fruitful and increase
> in number; fill the earth and subdue it. Rule over the fish
> in the sea and the birds in the sky and over every living
> creature that moves on the ground" (Genesis 1:26–28).

There is much debate about the meaning of *Imago Dei*, the Image of God. Some have adopted a substantive view thinking that the Image of God consists of a definite physical, psychological, or spiritual form like ours. Others have stressed a functional view giving primacy to what man does. Still others have adopted a relational view in which Jesus possesses the Image of God, and only those who have faith in him have been adopted into his image. Several people give credence to the Reformed view in which man's conscious propensities, i.e. knowledge, righteousness, holiness, and natural affections, best encompass God's image in us.

Whatever view one may favor, we can be certain that we're created in the image of the one who made us. And the one who made us is Elohim. How amazing is that! We were made in the similitude of one who is mighty and majestic. We've been given the power to manage what Elohim created. More than that, we have a dignified role in his creation. We exercise dominion over what God has made. Instilled within us are the power and majesty befitting ones like Elohim. We discover our true significance in our Creator. Eureka!

While we sense our insignificance amid his creation, we are uplifted, knowing that out of all the creatures on this earth, our being corresponds uniquely with our Creator. We're privileged to share to some degree in his awesome power and majesty. As he has created all things, we can procreate new life as males and females. As He rules over all creation, we exercise dominion over what he has made.

This truth should give comfort to our feelings of low self-esteem. Comparing ourselves with others may tempt us to feel inferior and insignificant. Others are smarter and more attractive. They're more talented: singing, dancing, writing, painting, and speaking are just a few examples of another's presumed superiority. They're leaders, kings and queens of the prom who're most likely to succeed and usually do. They can run faster and farther than you, easily shoot hoops, and pin an opponent in less than a minute. They win the prizes. You get honorable mention.

But here's the good news! Our self-worth isn't measured by these external factors as impressive as they may be. Instead, our value is rooted in the irrefutable fact that we were made in the same way as everyone else…in the image of Elohim. His image defines us. We are human beings precisely because the Imago Dei is infused within our whole being, our body, soul, and spirit. His image in us remains constant over time; it cannot diminish. The tiny unborn child just conceived and the elderly great-grandmother in hospice have the same worth as the thirty-five-year-old who works at Amazon, drives a Tesla, and has 1.5 children—and a dog. Praise Elohim for that!

At the same time as God lifts us up to the level of His image, he limits us to the boundaries of our humanity. God did not create other gods. He created humankind—which means the devil got it wrong. Genesis, chapter three, says that the serpent (aka the devil, Revelation 12:9) seduced the woman into believing that if she and her husband ate from the forbidden fruit of the tree of the knowledge of good and evil, their eyes would be opened, "and you will be like God, knowing good and evil" (Genesis 3:5). They fell for the devil's lies and ate of the fruit. The result…their eyes were opened, and they didn't see they were like God. They only saw that they were naked!

The image of God inscribed in us doesn't mean we're God's equal. Humanity isn't an extension or manifestation of the divine being. Nor do we have the potential to become divine ourselves. Instead, we've been uniquely designed in such a way that God's nature resonates in perfect harmony with ours. Our souls vibrate to the song of God's love for us.

If the Creator's intent were to make someone who can enjoy being in his presence and find ultimate joy and fulfillment in his companionship, then he would need to equip such beings with the moral, spiritual, and intellectual capacities to make good his desire. And, as it turns out, we are perfectly made to understand, appreciate, and respond to our maker's intentions.

My wife and I had a dog named Brinny. She was an incredibly ugly animal. She looked to me like a bat with four legs. Big bat-shaped ears rose above her head, and a tooth protruded from her upper lip. She sported a shabby short black and brown fur coat that shouted, "I am homeless!" She was, in fact, a fugitive from the Humane Society. But for all her shortcomings, Brinny was the most affectionate animal we've ever had. She'd race through the kitchen into the living room and jump on the coach where we were sitting. She'd nuzzle up to our sides and stay there until we went to bed.

As much as we enjoyed Brinny, there were many shortcomings as well. We could never share our deepest feelings with her. Carrying on a meaningful conversation with her was out of the question. When asked what she thought about our weekend travel plans, she'd look at us and say, "   ." Yep, nothing. And she meant it too.

Brinny wasn't wired for the kind of union a deep abiding fellowship requires. In contrast, God made divine-human relationships for fellowship. We come equipped with everything needed for a deep abiding relationship to flourish. This is the essence of what it means to be made in the image of Elohim (God). Amen!

CHAPTER 3
A SPECIAL MOMENT
(Yahweh)

IF YOU OFFERED to buy your teenager a pair of generic brand basketball shoes or the latest Nike Air Jordan XXXVI big kids' shoes, what do you think their choice might be? Hmmm…I wonder. Just a wild guess for Nike shoes. Why? Because popular name brands are special. They make you feel special. In fact, your feet feel special. You perform better when you play the game with Air Jordan empowerment. It's worth the extra one hundred dollars, right?

In Father Abraham's day, El was a generic word used to designate any god such as Hadad and Moloch. It falls within the generic genre of Theos in Greek and God in English. When harnessed and directed toward our God (the only God), the name El has a general all-purpose function: to identify God as the Almighty being.

When Isaac (Abraham's son) was about to die, he blessed his son Jacob (even after he tricked his father): "May God Almighty (El) bless you and make you fruitful and increase your numbers until you become a community of peoples" (Genesis 28:3). Years later, God himself spoke to Jacob and said, "I am God Almighty (El); be fruitful and increase in number. A nation and a community of nations will come from you, and kings will be among your descendants" (Genesis 35:11).

While El, Theos, and God are good names useful in a general sense, God has also chosen to reveal himself by names with a restricted function. These names were meant to convey a special relationship between himself and humankind. For example, when God spoke to Abram (soon to be renamed Abraham) and commissioned him to leave his country and travel to a foreign land, he revealed himself by a name not shared by Abram's relatives:

> The LORD (Yahweh)[2] has said to Abram, "Go from your country, your people and your father's household to the land I will show you. I will make you into a great nation, and I will bless you; I will make your name great, and you will be a blessing. I will bless those who bless you, and whoever curses you I will curse; and all peoples on earth will be blessed through you" (Genesis 12:1–3).

Imagine Abram joining his family for dinner at the end of that day. Once everyone was seated, Terah asked his son how his day went. In response, Abram told him that Yahweh appeared to him and told him to leave his country and family and travel to a foreign land. Yahweh also promised to make him into a great nation and that all the people on earth will be blessed through him. To this, Terah casually says, "That's nice, son. Pass the lamb chops."

I think Terah would be full of questions. Who is Yahweh? Where are you going? How long will you be gone? Are you sure he meant everyone will be blessed? Why did he choose you? And the questions would keep coming. Forget the lamb chops.

More importantly, how do you think Abram felt? Of all the people on the planet, God chose him to be a conduit for global blessing. Now that is special! This was a moment Abram could cherish for the rest of his life. Yahweh's special name fits in well with special unforgettable occasions. Feelings of

---

2   Refer to Appendix B for an explanation of how we have come to use the name "Yahweh" instead of its original name in Hebrew.

insignificance take a backseat when called by the Creator of the universe to accomplish his will.

If someone addressed me as Mr. Herring, I'd conclude they don't know me very well if at all personally. I'm just a name on a calling list or roster. "Mr. Herring, the doctor will see you now." If they called me "Jim," I'd assume they know me more personally. If I was called "Jimmy," I'd know that the one calling me is my brother or sister. "Jimmy" is a name given to a member of the family. The name "Yahweh" was a personal name of endearment shared from one family to the next. For centuries, Abraham, Isaac, Jacob, and all the family members who made up the nation of Israel addressed their God by the most personal and intimate name...."Yahweh."

Fast forward some 400 years and a lot of history after Abraham. A descendant by the name of Moses had an encounter of the amazing kind. A bush was on fire but wasn't consumed. Moses approached the fiery spectacle for a closer look. Suddenly God (Elohim) spoke to him from within the bush. God informed him that he was keenly aware of the suffering of his kinsmen the Israelites who had become slaves to Pharaoh. He then commissioned Moses to go to Pharaoh and take the people out of Egypt. In response, Moses said to God,

> "Suppose I go to the Israelites and say to them,
> 'The God of your fathers has sent me to you,' and
> they ask me, "What is his name?" 'Then what shall
> I tell them?' God said to Moses, "I AM WHO I
> AM. This is what you are to say to the Israelites:
> I AM has sent me to you" (Exodus 3:13–14).

"I AM WHO I AM" or "I AM" is the meaning of the name of Yahweh. It speaks of the LORD's self-existence. He is the self-sufficient, self-sustaining God. He who appeared to Moses as "I AM" is the God who appeared to Abraham centuries earlier as Yahweh. They are the same. One means the other.

God's Gift of Intimacy

The implication of God's personal name is both humbling and uplifting. God as Yahweh doesn't need anything to sustain him or complete him. He doesn't need anyone. He doesn't need you or me. Yikes! If that doesn't cause a spike in our sense of insignificance, I don't know what can.

This truth is also uplifting. Even though God as Yahweh doesn't need us, he chose to make himself known to us and to invest himself in our lives in the most personal of ways. He sees our needs and takes steps to deliver us out of whatever binds us. He chose a nation and gave the people his personal name that they may know him and love him with "all your heart and with all your soul and with all your strength" (Deuteronomy 6:4). Our sense of significance is rooted in another's self-sufficiency.

The personal name of Yahweh should be a badge of honor we'd want to wear proudly. Every chance we get, his name should grace our conversations and especially our communication with God. Sadly, however, we let our sense of insignificance get the upper hand. Out of reverence for all that is Holy, we return God's personal gift back to him marked unworthy to accept.

Eventually, the name Adonai was pressed into service and made to perform a double function. When speaking of God as our Lord and Master, the Hebrew people would use Adonai as this is what the name meant. But it was also used as a substitute whenever Yahweh was the subject in conversation and in writing.

So, how can anyone distinguish between these two functions? Several English translations of the Bible have incorporated a grammatical maneuver designed to alert the reader how Adonai was meant to be used. Notice the difference in the same word: Lord and LORD. In the first instance, only the first letter is in the upper case. This means that the name Adonai is used for its intended meaning. In the second instance, all the letters are in the upper case, which means that Adonai is used as a substitute for Yahweh. For example, in Exodus 4:10 (New International Version) we read, "Moses said to the **LORD**,

'Pardon your servant, **Lord**. I have never been eloquent, neither in the past nor since you have spoken to your servant. I am slow of speech and tongue."

Things become unnecessarily complicated when we depart from God's intended purposes. Our modern versions are not always helpful here. In Genesis 2:8–9, we read, "Now the **LORD God** had planted a garden in the east, in Eden; and there he put the man he had formed" (New International Version). But in Exodus 23:17 (New King James Version) it says, "Three times in the year all your males shall appear before the **Lord GOD**." What? In the first verse, the names in bold print refer to Yahweh and Elohim, but in the second verse, the words refer to Adonai and Yahweh. Wow! A general rule of thumb is that whenever the letters in the names Lord or God appear in all upper case, it is in reference to God's personal name Yahweh.

Enough said about the technicalities. There's no need to submit God's wonderful names to an unwarranted shell game. We're blessed to know God in a special and personal way. Rather than hesitate to embrace the name of God, we should take every opportunity to speak forth his name with praise and adoration. Every moment is special when we can address our Lord as Yahweh!

CHAPTER 4

MAKING WAR ON THE FLOOR

(El Elyon)

PICTURE YOUR RELATIVES taken captive by some unruly foes. These nasty fellows are far more numerous and powerful than you. Still, your heart's desire is to rescue the ones you love. But you aren't the strongest person on the block. What do you do?

This was somewhat the dilemma Abram faced when he left his homeland to relocate in the land promised by God and took his nephew Lot with him. Once settled in, both Abram and Lot chose different parcels of land in which to dwell. Unfortunately, at the same time and place several kings were engaged in tumultuous turf wars. Lot got caught up in the maelstrom, and several kings who had formed an alliance took him captive.

Abram heard about his nephew's predicament. In response, he marshalled 318 men and went to rescue him. In a special ops midnight attack, Abram and his men routed those who had taken Lot captive. Abram managed to rescue Lot along with his fellow captives and all their possessions.

On his return home, Abram encountered a most peculiar individual by the name of Melchizedek. He was the king of Salem. Most importantly, he was the priest of El Elyon, which means God Most High—the strongest one:

Then Melchizedek king of Salem brought out bread
and wine. He was priest of God Most High (El Elyon),
and he blessed Abram, saying, "Blessed be Abram by
God Most High, Creator of heaven and earth. And
praise be to God Most High, who delivered your
enemies into your hand" (Genesis 14:18-20).

Melchizedek and Abram met together at precisely the time when the
latter scored a major victory over superior forces. Rather than being a chance
encounter, this meeting was a divine appointment.

The context required clarification, and God appointed Melchizedek
to exposit the events for Abram. The victory can't be attributed to good
luck, smart thinking, courageous action, night vision goggles, or Apache
helicopters. Even if all these things were evidenced (minus the goggles and
helicopters), the outcome came as a direct result of El Elyon. He delivered
the enemies into Abram's hands. As strong as his enemies were, El Elyon
was the strongest. Although his enemies had assumed the high honor as
kings, El Elyon is the Most High. In short, Abram's enemies were no match
for El Elyon.

The Creator was not ruling on some distant planet, rearranging con-
stellations in the heavens as a show of his strength. No, He was keenly aware
of the drama unfolding in Abram's life. At precisely the right moment, God
stepped in and provided just what was needed.

This should be a source of comfort and assurance to all of us. Numerous
times we feel helpless to deal with forces stronger than us. We don't possess
the inner strength or social position to make a difference. Victory seems as
far away as God must be. But Abram's experience tells us a different story.
If God is aware of one man's situation and can make a difference in his life,
surely he is aware of everyone's circumstances, and as El Elyon, he can make
a difference in all our lives. If he can do one, he can do the other.

Let's be clear though that God isn't at our beck and call. He's no cosmic genie slavishly resigned to answer our requests. God sovereignly delivered Abram and determined the meaning of what victory would mean for him at that point in time. Victory for us may not be what we ask God for but rather what God defines for us. The path to victory is a life lived out in faith trusting in his will for our lives. In any and all cases, God remains El Elyon the Most High...the Strongest.

The outworking of God's victorious work in Abram's life was twofold. First, it was intended to bring blessing to Abram, "Blessed be Abram by El Elyon." God meant victory to be an avenue whereby he bestowed a favor or gift upon Abram resulting in joy and happiness. To bless someone is an indication that we care for others and seek the best for them. That is just what took place between El Elyon and Abram.

The other effect of God's victorious work through Abram was to evoke praises on the part of the one who has been blessed: "praise be to El Elyon." If there was no way human beings could return the favor to the Most High, then the blessing would always be one-sided. We would be deprived of any ability to show our gratitude, to meaningfully express our tender regard for those who care deeply for us. Praise is that human capacity to express our highest regard for who God is and what he has accomplished in our lives. Intimacy always travels best and farthest on a two-way street.

And then there was Melchizedek. He held both austere positions as king and priest and yet he took upon himself the role of servant by bringing food and drink to refresh Abram who held neither position. This brings to light the pattern of humble intimacy: the greater, Melchizedek served the lesser who was Abram.

In the New Testament, this pattern is finally and perfectly established in Jesus, God's only begotten Son. To the believers at Philippi, the Apostle Paul wrote,

THE GREATEST PRESENCE OF ALL

> "In your relationships with one another, have the same
> mindset as Christ Jesus: Who, being in very nature
> God, did not consider equality with God something to
> be used to his own advantage; rather, he made himself
> nothing by taking the very nature of a servant, being
> made in human likeness. And being found in appearance
> as a man, he humbled himself by becoming obedient to
> death—even death on a cross!" (Philippians 2:5–8).

Jesus who was and is the greatest as God, serves the lesser humankind by becoming the least among men, a humble servant. And if that was not enough, he willingly died the most horrific death imaginable, death by crucifixion. One cannot fully understand the extent God went to bring us closer to himself.

The night before he was crucified, Jesus reinforced the pattern of the greater serving the lesser. In the upper room, Jesus performed a ritual as an unforgettable object lesson:

> Jesus knew that the Father had put all things under
> his power, and that he had come from God and was
> returning to God; so he got up from the meal, took
> off his outer clothing, and wrapped a towel around
> his waist. After that, he poured water into a basin and
> began to wash his disciples' feet drying them with the
> towel that was wrapped around him (John 13:3–4).

His disciples, jostling back and forth to determine who was the greatest among them, needed further insight into the ritual they had just experienced. To help them understand, Jesus said to them,

> "I have set you an example that you should do as I have
> done for you. Very truly I tell you, no servant is greater
> than his master, nor is a messenger greater than the

26

one who sent him. Now that you know these things,
you will be blessed if you do them" (John 13:15–17).

If Jesus, who is greater than his disciples served them, they too must follow his example of the greater serving the lesser.

During the five years my wife and I visited Terre Blanch in Haiti, several Haitian men and women were hired to take care of our physical needs. The men stayed up at night and walked around the compound providing security for us and our team of high school students. They also travelled back and forth from the nearby town of Gonaives with supplies. The women cooked our meals, cleaned the rooms we occupied, and even hand-washed our laundry down at the river.

The night before we left for home, we asked if those who served us would be our guests of honor at an evening celebration. Those who had served us sat on chairs lined up at the front of the room in the basement of the compound. Each student had a basin of water and a towel. The students got down on their knees on the floor and poured water over feet that literally walked miles to take care of us. They gently took towels and wiped the earth-hardened feet of our caretakers.

During the ceremony, I happened to look around at the many Haitian people who had filled the room. I saw those in the back standing up to take a closer look at what the students were doing. Many people were moved to tears at what they saw. Jesus was right. Those who follow his example are the ones who are truly blessed!

It's important to put things in perspective. As El Elyon, God is deserving of all honor and glory from his creation. He is enthroned in heaven for a reason! At the same time, God is also willing to set aside his regal privilege temporarily and assume the role of a servant to bring into his presence those whom he has created. Both sides of this coin are in play.

Scripture helps us to balance these complimentary truths. It's true that Christ bent his knee to wash the feet of his disciples. It's also true that

God exalted him to the highest place and gave
him the name that is above every name, that at the
name of Jesus every knee should bow, in heaven
and on earth and under the earth, and every tongue
acknowledge that Jesus Christ is Lord, to the
glory of God the Father (Philippians 2:9–11).

The greater who blessed the lesser is indeed the Greatest. Blessed be the name of El Elyon!

CHAPTER 5

WHAT A DIFFERENCE A NAME MAKES
(El Roi and El Shaddai)

I'M REMINDED OF an advertisement that tried to demonstrate the difference between two cell phone companies. The salesman held up two maps of the US showing the extent of coverage for each cell phone service. One coverage cost more than the other, and the maps themselves were in different colors. What was most revealing was the fact that the coverage for these two companies was the same. Aside from paying more for one service than another (along with a nifty colored map), neither company's coverage made any difference to the consumer. By contrast, the names God reveals to us are intended to show that his presence makes a transformative difference in our lives. The following two names more than accomplish this task.

YOU ARE EL ROI...

Faith is both an individual and a family affair. Not everyone in a relationship is at the same level of faith. Take for example Abram and his wife Sarai. God appeared to Abram in a vision and said to him, "Look up at the sky and count the stars—if indeed you can count them.' Then he said to him, 'So shall your offspring be'" (Genesis 15:5). In response we read, "Abram believed the LORD, and he credited it to him as righteousness" (15:6). By contrast Sarai,

Abram's wife, had borne him no children. But she had an Egyptian slave named Hagar, so she said to Abram, "The LORD has kept me from having children. Go, sleep with my slave; perhaps I can build a family through her" (Genesis 16:2).

Sarai wrongfully concluded that because she had remained childless for years, God must not want her to play a starring role in bringing a child into the world. Since culture allowed for a childless woman to have her slave act as a surrogate, this must be what God had in mind. Thus, Sarai set in motion a course of action that would have negative repercussions for generations to come.

Hagar's pregnancy gave birth to a whole host of hurt feelings between all parties concerned. How could it not? Feelings became so explosive Hagar ran away from Sarai. At a nearby spring in the desert the angel of the LORD spoke to her: "Hagar, slave of Sarai, where have you come from, and where are you going?' 'I'm running away from my mistress Sarai,' she answered" (Genesis 16:8). The angel encouraged her to return to Sarai with the promise that God would bless her with many descendants. In response to the angel, Hagar gave the LORD a name: "You are the God who sees me (El Roi)" (Genesis 16:13).

While it may be tempting to think that God reserves his attention for those who are important, who make a difference in society, this passage delivers a different message. God has his eye (figuratively speaking) on the Patriarch, the Princess (the meaning of Saria), and the slave girl. No one is excluded from His watchfulness. Everyone is important to God. He sees us all.

The Psalmist echoed these same sentiments: "From heaven the LORD looks down and sees all mankind; from his dwelling place he watches all who live on earth—he who forms the hearts of all, who considers everything they do" (Psalm 33:13–14). The God who made the stars also formed our hearts. He hasn't lost sight of any beating heart in all of creation. How amazing!

The Son, like the Father, demonstrated this as well. Jesus did not hobnob (a good theological term) with only the social, political, and religious elites.

Instead, he intentionally spent time with those society had rejected. He hung out with the outsiders: tax collectors, fishermen, and women of ill repute. He even touched the untouchables. Jesus saw the hurt, the pain, and the guilt. And he did something about it. He made a difference.

It's not enough that El Roi happened to see where Hagar was. God saw her desperate situation. He could see what she needed to do in the present moment, and He saw what would happen to her in the future: "Go back to your mistress and submit to her." The angel added, "I will increase your descendants so much that they will be too numerous to count." The angel of the LORD also said to her, "You are now pregnant and you will give birth to a son. You shall name him Ishmael, for the LORD has heard of your misery" (Genesis 16:9–11).

Sometimes we feel like we're invisible. It's one thing to see us. It's another to see our misery. It's even more significant to see what we need now and in the future. It would be a hard sell to convince people that we want to build a meaningful relationship with them when we have no grasp of what they're going through. Fortunately, we aren't invisible to God. He sees what we're going through and wants to go through it together with us. That's insight that makes a difference. Praise be to El Roi!

I AM EL SHADDAI...

Thirteen years passed since Ishmael was born to Hagar. Abram was nearly one hundred years old, and Sarah (previously named Sarai) was ninety. The physical strength and vitality sufficient for them to have a son of their own had slipped away. It would have been silly to think that they could become parents: "Abraham fell facedown; he laughed and said to himself, 'Will a son be born to a man a hundred years old? Will Sarah bear a child at the age of ninety?'" (Genesis 17:17). This, however, was about to change.

God appeared to Abram again and revealed himself by a new name:

When Abram was ninety-nine years old, the LORD
appeared to him and said, "I am God Almighty (El
Shaddai); walk before me faithfully and be blameless.
Then I will make my covenant between me and you and
will greatly increase your numbers" (Genesis 17:1–2).

Note the contrasts. Abram was ninety-nine years old. No physical regimen could wipe away a century of time that had taken a toll on Abram's body. Having a child biologically was simply out of the question. But what about God? Did he grow old alongside Abram? Perhaps the LORD had moved into an assisted living mansion in heaven. Just imagine the sight—Abram hobbling about with a cane and God clutching a celestial walker. Both reminiscing about the good old days over a glass of warm milk.

This isn't the scene. God appears as El Shaddai. He is God Almighty—All Sufficient. Abram got old and weak, not God. In contrast to Abram whose time had passed, it was exactly the right time for El Shaddai to act. God's strength remained absolute and undiminished over time. It wasn't what Abram could or couldn't do with age. It was about what God can do with infinite power.

Having a child was an impossible task for a centenarian, but not for El Shaddai. God is in the business of making the impossible possible. When God shows up, things happen. God makes a difference.

God wasn't just into bodybuilding, reinvigorating a body to engage in procreation. He was also deeply involved in faith building. Consider what the Apostle Paul said about Abram's faith.

Without weakening in his faith, he faced the fact that
his body was as good as dead—since he was about a
hundred years old—and that Sarah's womb was also
dead. Yet he did not waver through unbelief regarding
the promise of God, but was strengthened in his faith and

gave glory to God, being fully persuaded that God had
power to do what he had promised (Romans 4:19–21).

We can also see the contrast between Abram and El Shaddai by the demands he placed on Abram. God didn't tell him to start exercising or watching his diet. No, God told him to "walk before me faithfully and be blameless" (Genesis 17:1). The dynamic ingredient sufficient to build a lasting relationship between God and humankind is faithfulness that produces blamelessness, a life that honors God. All who desire to walk with God must have the kind of faith that changes the way they walk before God.

To reinforce his covenant promises, El Shaddai changed both Abram's and Sarai's names. Concerning Abram: "No longer will you be called Abram; your name will be Abraham, for I have made you a father of many nations" (Genesis 17:5). As for Abram's wife:

> "[Y]ou are no longer to call her Sarai; her name will be
> Sarah. I will bless her and will surely give you a son by her.
> I will bless her so that she will be the mother of nations;
> kings of peoples will come from her" (Genesis 17:15–16).

Abram meant "exalted father." Abraham meant "father of a multitude." Likewise, Sarai meant "my princess." Sarah meant "a princess, namely of many." God promised he would make Abram and Sarai the parents of many nations. Here, God changed their names to match the promise. Names do make a difference!

Sarah's response matched Abraham's. In the following chapter, God visited Abraham again and reiterated the promise that Sarah will bear a son. Overhearing this, "Sarah laughed to herself as she thought, 'After I am worn out and my lord is old, will I now have this pleasure?'" (Genesis 18:12).

Perhaps their laughter was a mix of wonder and unbelief at the prospect of becoming parents so late in life. In any event, God was fully aware of their emotional state. We know this from the name they were to give to the son of the promise: "…your wife Sarah will bear you a son, and you will call him

Isaac. I will establish my covenant with him as an everlasting covenant for his descendants after him" (Genesis 17:19). Isaac means laughter! God made the name of the son match the emotional state of his parents.

Sarah's laughter of unbelief before giving birth gave way to the laughter of exuberant joy once Isaac was born. As we read in Scripture, "Sarah became pregnant and bore a son to Abraham in his old age, at the very time God had promised him…Sarah said, 'God has brought me laughter, and everyone who hears about this will laugh with me" (Genesis 21:2, 6).

God doesn't depend upon emojis to provide emotional cues missing from his relationship with us. His presence is sufficient to fulfill his promises to us and to fill our souls' otherwise emotional deficit. This is far and away better than a happy face!

Our feelings are important to God. He takes note of our laughter and tears. And he does something about it. The Psalmist, beloved for expressing how we feel, wrote,

> The LORD is close to the brokenhearted and saves
> those who are crushed in spirit. The righteous person
> may have many troubles, but the LORD delivers
> him from them all; he protects all his bones, not
> one of them will be broken (Psalm 34:18–19).

God is not indifferent to our feelings. He's never closer to us than when our hearts are broken and we feel the crushing weight of despair. Just as he heals our broken bones, he can and does heal our broken hearts. As El Shaddai, he is sufficient to make a difference in our lives.

CHAPTER 6
FROM HERE TO ETERNITY
(EL OLAM)

CAN YOU NAME something that has always existed just as it is, functioned in the same way, maintained its original value over time, and can't be replaced or duplicated by anything better than what it is? I have a cell phone that's over ten years old. It still functions in the same way, but I've been notified that it needs replacement by something more efficient—something to do with gigabytes. I had to replace my laptop because it was acting more like a refrigerator than a computer—constantly freezing in mid-function. I found a rare Indian trade token (more on this later) that has increased in value, but there was a time when it didn't exist. Nope, I can't think of anything.

Well, if I can't think of any candidate for the above requirements, Abraham did. Having been around for a hundred years, old Abe summed up what he'd learned about God by addressing Him with a new name: "Abraham planted a tamarisk tree in Beersheba, and there he called on the name of the LORD, the Eternal God" (Genesis 21:33). Here, Abraham addressed God by the name of El Olam, which means The Everlasting God.

Abraham had lived long enough to hold in his hands the son God gave him in his old age. His feet had walked the land the LORD had promised to give him. God had prospered, protected, and provided for him. In response

35

THE GREATEST PRESENCE OF ALL

to all these blessings, Abraham had learned that the one in whom he had placed his trust was and is the eternal, constant, and unique being—El Olam!

I've received many gifts over the last seventy-four years. Most of these didn't last very long. They wore out, broke down, couldn't function, or I lost interest in them. But what wonderful gifts El Olam has in store for those who walk with him!

God's eternal capacities infuse his gifts. This means that because God is El Olam, his gifts aren't bound by temporal parameters. He doesn't provide only for our mortal needs. The eternal God blesses us with gifts pertaining to eternity.

That Abraham was aware of this fundamental truth is evident in several places in Scripture. First, for the entire time Abraham and his immediate descendants lived in the land of promise, they continued to live in tents. No one built permanent structures, houses, or cities. Why? We read:

> By faith he made his home in the promised land like a stranger in a foreign country; he lived in tents, as did Isaac and Jacob, who were heirs with him of the same promise. For he was looking forward to the city with foundations, whose architect and builder is God (Hebrews 11:9–10).

Abraham believed that God, who had promised him and his descendants a land to dwell in, would also build them a place to live. The city he was looking for wasn't just a physical structure but a social institution, a place where all who are heirs of the promise may live and flourish.

Abraham's son and grandson shared his vision of God's eternal blessings as well. They had lived long enough to enjoy some aspects of the promise such as the birth of Abraham's son, living in the promised land, and being materially blessed. Other aspects such as a city, many nations, and the coming of the Messiah awaited future fulfillment. They continued to trust God knowing that he, being eternal, has eternity to fulfill his promises.

God's Gift of Intimacy

Abraham learned early on that neither God nor his promises can be limited to time and space. This was an important truth he didn't keep to himself. Isaac and Jacob also lived in the truths their father Abraham had taught them. Unfortunately, a new generation of teachers arose over time who didn't share his eternal perspective.

For example, the leaders in Jesus's day tried to expose him as an ignorant blasphemer. They concocted dilemmas they thought would confound this wayward son of a carpenter. Surely, he wasn't educated like they were to grasp the many nuances of the law as they could. But try as they might, they failed to accomplish their goal.

Finally, a group of political elitists called the Sadducees came up with what they thought was a surefire plan to expose this charlatan. They laid out before Jesus a complicated maze of relationships guaranteed to tie him up in theological knots. To summarize (see Matthew 22:23–28), a woman was married seven times and finally died. In the resurrection, they asked, who would she be married to?

Jesus knew that the Sadducees were secularists and didn't believe in the resurrection at all. The question was mute. Once you're dead, it's all over. They also considered only the first five books of Moses as Scripture and therefore authoritative. They believed Moses never spoke about the resurrection. Therefore, there was no scriptural warrant for belief in life after death.

In response, Jesus said to them,

> "But about the resurrection of the dead—have you not read what God said to you, 'I am the God of Abraham, the God of Isaac, and the God of Jacob'? He is not the God of the dead but of the living" (Matthew 22:32).

Jesus told them that in light of the resurrection, the patriarchs were literally alive and not dead. Furthermore, the Scripture Jesus used as a proof text for the resurrection was taken from Exodus 3:6,15—the very heart of the Scriptures the Sadducees claimed didn't support the doctrine of the

resurrection. Jesus was certainly right to rebuke them for their gross igno-
rance of Scripture: "You are in error because you do not know the Scriptures
or the power of God" (Matthew 22: 29).

Not only did Moses write about the resurrection, three of Jesus's own
disciples saw Moses himself alive from the dead. Jesus had taken Peter, James,
and John to a mountain. At the top, Jesus's appearance was transfigured. At
that very moment, "there appeared before them Moses and Elijah talking with
Jesus" (Mathew 17:3). Here, Jesus had a conversation with two outstanding
Old Testament figures—all of them very much alive!

As it turned out, Abraham was right to take God's promises literally. He
and his descendants after him would indeed live to see God's eternal blessings
come to pass. And we can trust in El Olam to fulfill his promises to us as well.

God desires to be with us and lavish upon us his many blessings. A paltry
one hundred years is just not enough time to work in all that God has in store
for us. In response to his many blessings, we will need eternity to express our
gratitude to Him. As Paul exclaimed,

> "Oh, the depth of the riches of the wisdom and
> knowledge of God! How unsearchable his judgments,
> and his paths beyond tracing out!...For from Him
> and through Him and for him are all things. To him
> be glory forever! Amen" (Romans 11:33, 36).

CHAPTER 7

WHAT A PLACE! WHAT A NAME!

(Yahweh Yireh)

MY BROTHER AND I were Boy Scouts growing up in Colorado. Our troop of about twenty boys and their fathers went backpacking in the high Rocky Mountains on a regular basis throughout the summer. On one trip, the Scout Master and his son were setting up their tent. Suddenly, the father started yelling at his son about something he was responsible to bring with him…it was their sleeping bags! The son had left behind a much-needed provision for the trip. They ended up lying on the ground inside the tent, freezing all night!

When Isaac was about fourteen years old, God tested Abraham's faith: "Take your son, your only son, whom you love---Isaac---and go to the region of Moriah. Sacrifice him there as a burnt offering on a mountain I will show you" (Genesis 22:2).[3] Abraham cut the wood, prepared food and water, and took two of his servants along with Isaac and headed out.

As Isaac and Abraham proceeded up the mountain, Isaac, who apparently was familiar with sacrificial offerings, became aware that something was missing and brought it to his father's attention. "Father?' 'Yes, my son?'

---

[3] Some people see this command as a contradiction of the nature and purposes of a loving God. I recommend Paul Copan's defense of God's character considering this and other related problems in his book, *Is God a Moral Monster?* (Particularly chapter five: "Child Abuse and Bullying? God's Ways and the Binding of Isaac.")

39

Abraham replied. 'The fire and wood are here,' Isaac said, 'but where is the lamb for the burnt offering?'" (Genesis 22:7). Abraham had provided for everything but the thing he needed the most—the sacrificial lamb!

Sometimes we spend a great deal of time getting the peripheral things in order and lose sight of what's essential. Take for example all that goes into a church service in Your Town, USA. A fully equipped and staffed espresso bar is standard fare. Nursery care is a must. Separate age-graded services are essential. Parishioners expect the best musicians and vocalists. Multiple worship services cater to early and late risers. The latest sound and computer systems are needed. And, especially in the wake of Covid, people should be able to choose to attend a live service or stay at home and watch it online. Hopefully, everyone will like us on Facebook.

What about the preaching and teaching of the Word of God? It's been relegated to a twenty-minute add-on that comes across semi-convincing and relevant only by virtue of the many anecdotes the audience can identify with. Heavy on the jokes and light on conviction. Not too deep or you'll lose the average occasional church attender.

I know this is one-sided, but it is one side of the bread many churches butter their church services on. Too many churches go out of their way providing things that aren't essential for spiritual growth. All the while, God is more than prepared to provide what we really need.

This was the crucial moment when Abraham appealed to God as the ultimate provider. In response to Isaac's query, Abraham replied, "God himself will provide the lamb for the burnt offering, my son" (Genesis 22:8). Regardless of what might happen on the mountain, Abraham was convinced God would provide what was essential for the sacrifice to take place.

It's important to keep in mind that two things took place on the mountain: a faith test and a sacrifice. They overlapped one another, and yet Abraham saw the distinction between them. By faith, Abraham offered up his son Isaac as the means by which he could demonstrate his faith. Only God could provide

God's Gift of Intimacy

a sacrifice sufficient to make atonement for man's sin. The moment Abraham's faith had been revealed, the sacrifice also became manifest:

> Then he reached out his hand and took the knife to slay his son. But the angel of the LORD called out to him from heaven, "Abraham! Abraham!" "Here I am," he replied. "Do not lay a hand on the boy," he said. "Do not do anything to him. Now I know that you fear God, because you have not withheld from me your son, your only son." Abraham looked up and there in a thicket he saw a ram caught by its horns. He went over and took the ram and sacrificed it as a burnt offering instead of his son (Genesis 22:10–13).

In response to the LORD's provision, Abraham "called that place The LORD Will Provide. And to this day it is said, 'On the mountain of the LORD it will be provided'" (Genesis 22:14). The LORD Will Provide is the meaning of the name Yahweh Yireh. The name matched the place. Where faith and sacrifice meet, you will always find the Lord there to provide what's needed. What a place! What a name!

God brings to a relationship the resources to meet our deepest needs. Not only did Abraham witness this, so did his descendants. In the wilderness, Moses reminded Abraham's lineage,

> "The LORD your God has blessed you in all the work of your hands. He has watched over your journey through this vast wilderness. These forty years the LORD your God has been with you, and you have not lacked anything" (Deuteronomy 2:7).

The Apostle Paul, like Moses before him, reminded believers of the same enduring truth. To the believers at Philippi he said, "And my God will meet all your needs according to the riches of his glory in Christ Jesus" (Philippians 4:19). Surely, God is with us to provide for us.

This all sounds great, but what about those who are neither one of Abraham's descendants nor a bona fide member of a local church? Does a person have to belong to the Good Old Boys Club to qualify for one of God's many provisions? The answer is yes and no.

Many of God's provisions are only for those who desire to be in a personal relationship with God through his Son Jesus Christ. Speaking about Christ, the Apostle John said,

> He came to that which was his own, but his own
> did not receive him. Yet to all who did receive him,
> to those who believed in his name, he gave the
> right to become children of God—children born
> not of natural descent, nor of human decision or a
> husband's will, but born of God (John 1:11–13).

Becoming a part of God's eternal family and enjoying all the rights as an heir to God's kingdom is open to all who would receive Christ as God's only begotten Son. This same person must also believe that Jesus died on the cross to pay the penalty for our sins and that he was buried and then rose from the dead on the morning of the third day (see 1 Corinthians 15:3 and Romans 10:9–10). But if a person chooses not to receive and believe in this way, he can't claim the provisions that come with being a part of God's eternal family.

But this doesn't exclude a person from benefitting from all of God's provisions. When the Apostles Paul and Barnabas took the Gospel (good news) of Christ out to the world, they encountered many people raised in a pagan religion. They weren't familiar with God's promises to Abraham, and they had no clue who Jesus was. That being said, Christ's disciples were quick to point out that God had been providing for them their whole lives: "…He has shown kindness by giving you rain from heaven and crops in their seasons; he provides you with plenty of food and fills your hearts with joy" (Acts 14:17).

The Creator of heaven and earth takes care of his creation. He has provided what is sufficient and necessary for his creatures both small and great

God's Gift of Intimacy

to flourish physically. He has also provided for those who were created in his image to thrive spiritually as well. God is the provider of both. We who have always benefitted from God's physical blessings must choose to receive his spiritual blessings.

Those who have responded by faith to God's immeasurable provision in his Son Jesus Christ are truly blessed indeed. As Scripture declares, "Praise be to the God and Father of our Lord Jesus Christ, who has blessed us in the heavenly realms with every spiritual blessing in Christ" (Ephesians 1:3). Praise be to Yahweh Yireh, our great provider!

CHAPTER 8

INTO THE WILDERNESS

(Yahweh Rapha, Yahweh Nissi, Yahweh M'Kaddesh)

PROMISES, PROMISES, PROMISES. God promised a land, a people, and a seed by which to bless not just Abraham and his immediate descendants, but all people in every nation on earth (see Genesis 12:1–3). The problem was and is, are we ready to live the life God promised us?

After spending four hundred years in hard labor serving the kings of Egypt, the people were ready to be set free. And with the coming of Moses, that's exactly what happened. Instead of leading the people of Israel along the established trade routes to the promised land of Canaan, God led them into the wilderness. It was here in a desert setting that their faith would be tested, and the score card was less than impressive.

At almost every point in the wilderness, the people complained and grumbled as they slowly approached the promised land. They grumbled about the lack of food and water, about their leaders, and about the people they encountered. They even complained about God himself (see Exodus 15:22–25, 16:1–3, 8, 17:3–4; Numbers 14:2–4, 27). God brought all this to light within two to three weeks' march into the wilderness.

It all came to a head at a place called Kadesh-Barnea, an oasis south of Canaan. The people were poised to enter the land God had promised, but before entering en masse, Moses and the leaders of the people sent twelve men to spy out the land. Upon their return, they reported what they had encountered:

> "We went into the land to which you sent us, and
> it does flow with milk and honey! Here is its fruit.
> But the people who live there are powerful, and
> the cities are fortified and very large. We even saw
> descendants of Anak there" (Numbers 13:27–28).

The promised land was flowing with milk and honey—and giants!

Most people are ready for milk and honey, an expression of abundance. Facing giants is another matter. The promised land had both. Not only had the children of Israel grumbled at God all the way to Kadesh-Barnea, but they were also not ready for **all** the promised land had to offer: "We should choose a leader and go back to Egypt" (Numbers 14:4). The children of Israel would rather go back into slavery in Egypt than go forward and trust God to conquer their giants.

If the people would not go with God into the promised land, God would continue to go with them into the wilderness. Although it was not a land flowing with milk and honey, it would be a place to prepare a people to live within the borders of God's promises.

In the wilderness, God continued to reveal himself in ways that would help them go through the refining furnace and come out a people equipped for life in the promised land. The Lord chiseled the following names of God on hearts that would one day beat in rhythm to His presence.

Yahweh Rapha

God had sent Moses to free the children of Abraham and lead them out of Egypt, but Pharoah had hardened his heart against God and wouldn't let them

THE GREATEST PRESENCE OF ALL

go. In response, God worked through Moses and Aaron his brother to afflict the people of Egypt with many plagues. Once he witnessed this onslaught of sickness and death, Pharoah relented and let God's people go.

After only a few days travel in the wilderness, the people became thirsty. But when they reached Marah (which means bitter), they couldn't quench their thirst in the spring because of its foul taste. This brought to the surface a heart that had not yet tasted the sweet goodness of God. Rather than seek God out in prayer and supplication, "the people grumbled against Moses, saying, 'What are we to drink?'" (Exodus 15:24).

Here's where they encountered the healing hand of God. Rather than lead them to another place, God instructed Moses to throw a piece of wood into the water that would heal its bitterness. Moses did what God told him to do, and immediately the water became fit to drink (see Exodus 15:25).

This object lesson had a powerful application:

> "If you listen carefully to the LORD your God and
> do what is right in his eyes, if you pay attention to his
> commands and keep all his decrees, I will not bring
> on you any of the diseases I brought on the Egyptians,
> for I am the LORD, who heals you" (Exodus 15:26).

"The LORD who heals you" is the meaning of the name Yahweh Rapha. Just as God had healed the water, he could also heal their bitter hearts and keep them from the life-threatening plagues that befell the hard-hearted Egyptians.

God's people have come to know and experience the two sides of God's grace. He not only forgives us when we've rebelled against Him and repent, but he also heals us of the effects of rebelliousness in our lives. He's promised to do both: "Praise the LORD, my soul, and forget not all his benefits—who forgives all your sins and heals all your diseases" (Psalm 103:2–3).

Jesus demonstrated the power of God to both forgive and heal as he ministered to Abraham's descendants. At the beginning of his public ministry, people brought a paralytic to him to heal. Unable to access his presence, they ingeniously tore the shingles of the roof off the house in which Jesus resided and lowered the afflicted man down to him by ropes. Seeing such determined faith, Jesus said to the paralytic, "Son, your sins are forgiven" (Mark 2:5).

The men who brought the paralytic to Jesus got more than they bargained for. The first and most important thing Jesus did was to forgive the paralytic. This didn't sit well with the Jewish leadership. They knew that only God could forgive sins (2:6–7). Knowing their bitter unbelieving hearts, Jesus proceeded to heal the paralytic as a demonstration of what had been revealed centuries beforehand to the people in the wilderness: God as Yahweh Rapha has the power to heal and to forgive.

Just as God performed heart surgery at Marah to heal bitter hearts, he can heal us of our afflictions. God in Jesus is our Great Physician. We walk day by day with the world's most renowned heart surgeon. Praise be to Yahweh-Rapha!

Yahweh-Nissi

Even before they were given the opportunity to enter the promised land, the people of Israel faced a powerful enemy. The Amalekites were a seminomadic people who lived near the southern borders of the promised land. Seeing this massive people group coming out of Egypt may have posed a threat or possibly inspired the Amalekites to take advantage of this seemingly ragtag parade of misfits. They were ripe for easy pickings…or so they thought.

The Amalekites took note of the vulnerability of the Israelites. They could see that due to a lack of water and constant travel, the people became weak and exhausted. The elderly and those who couldn't keep up lagged behind. At a place called Rephidim, a desert place with no natural water resources to refresh them, the Amalekites attacked. Not only were the Amalekites treacherous people, but they also refused to recognize that God was with the Israelites to protect them. As Moses reminded the children of Israel years later,

> "Remember what the Amalekites did to you along
> the way when you came out of Egypt. When you
> were weary and worn out, they met you on your
> journey and attacked all who were lagging behind;
> they had no fear of God" (Deuteronomy 25:17–18).

No matter how strong and clever the Amalekites thought they were, disregarding the Lord by thinking they could defeat his children was a bad idea.

Israel's battle plan was unconventional, to say the least. As it turned out, they fought the battle on two fronts: "So Joshua fought the Amalekites as Moses had ordered, and Moses, Aaron and Hur went to the top of the hill" (Exodus 17:10).

One group engaged in hand-to-hand combat; the other engaged in senior aerobics. Moses lifted his shepherd's staff in the air. What? Surely there was no connection between these groups, but Scripture reveals otherwise. We read, "As long as Moses held up his hands, the Israelites were winning, but whenever he lowered his hands, the Amalekites were winning" (17:11). This takes Peloton to a whole new level!

With the help of Aaron and Hur, Moses remained steadfast on the hill, and Joshua won the battle against the Amalekites. To memorialize their victory, "Moses built an altar and called it The LORD is my Banner" (Exodus 17:15). Moses understood what the Amalekites failed to recognize: the God of Israel is Yahweh Nissi, the LORD is my Banner.

In battle, there is a banner bearer. This person is responsible to hold up a flag mounted on a pole. It often contained some insignia representing the army. The banner bearer is at the front leading the charge. Seeing the banner held up high reminds the army of what they stand for and motivates them to fight on.

By raising his staff, Moses acted as God's banner bearer. He is Yahweh Nissi, the one who protected Israel and gave them victory in battle. In the same way, the God who travels with us into our wilderness can bring us victory not only when we are strong, rested, and prepared. He protects us when we are exhausted, weak, and vulnerable. The same God who walks with those in the front of the battle also lifts those who have fallen behind. He cares for and walks with all his children. As Yahweh Nissi, his banner is over **all** of us.

Yahweh M'Kaddesh

When you read about all the laws and commandments recorded in Scripture, you might be tempted to think that God works from the outside in. To bring about change that glorifies God requires obedience to extrinsic requirements. God, it would seem, is mainly concerned with curb appeal. If you do what it says in a book, then you'll look the part and be acceptable to the Lord. The most that can be expected of us is that our behavior corresponds to written requirements. It's all skin deep.

But as the children wandered further into the wilderness, it became clear that God didn't desire mere window dressing. He doesn't want us to look the part. He desires that we live the part. In fact, he intends for us to be like him: to be set apart from all that doesn't honor him and be consecrated only to Him. God wants us to be holy like he is. That was precisely what God intended for the children of Israel as we read in Scripture, "consecrate yourselves and be holy, because I am the LORD your God" (Leviticus 20:7).

To be holy like God requires a realignment of expectations. God doesn't require outward patterns of worship and obedience to a written code of conduct. A meaningful relationship between God and man demands a radical spiritual transformation resulting in a life that desires harmony with God. The basic expectation of holiness is a life devoted to the life of another. Holiness then, works from the inside out producing patterns of behavior that beat in rhythm to God's being. It's a life that resists the temptation to accommodate

THE GREATEST PRESENCE OF ALL

patterns of thought and practice that would in any way harm the music of divine embrace.

The problem with the people of Israel (and us) is that as much as they'd detested being enslaved, they had deeply imbibed the culture and religion of their oppressors. How do we know this? Notice that when Moses went up to the mountain to meet with God he didn't return right away. In fact, he stayed on the mountain forty days and nights (see Exodus 24:18).

In his absence, what did the people do? Did they remain steadfast in their devotion to God and resist actions that would dishonor him? No! We read: "When the people saw that Moses was so long in coming down from the mountain, they gathered around Aaron and said, 'Come, make us gods who will go before us'" (Exodus 32:1). So, in response, Aaron made a golden calf out of the jewelry they brought out of Egypt.

Moses wasn't aware of what the people had done, but God certainly was. He told Moses,

> "Go down, because your people, whom you brought
> up out of Egypt, have become corrupt. They have been
> quick to turn away from what I commanded them
> and have made themselves an idol cast in the shape
> of a calf. They have bowed down to it and sacrificed
> to it and have said, 'These are your gods, Israel, who
> brought you up out of Egypt'" (Exodus 32:7–8).

The people whom God brought out of Egypt resorted to the behavior of the Egyptians and practiced idolatry just as they had seen their oppressors do for centuries. This is the exact opposite of what it means to be holy!

God revealed by his name what the people needed to bring them into proper alignment with himself: "Keep my decrees and follow them. I am the LORD, who makes you holy" (Leviticus 20:8). The LORD who makes you holy is the meaning of the name Yahweh M'Kaddesh. Decrees enlighten us

50

about what God desires, but God's intimate presence in our lives gives us the inner desire to want to follow his decrees in the first place.

Moses invested forty days and nights on the mountain with God, and the people thought it was too long to wait. However, God was willing to spend forty years in the wilderness to produce a people willing to follow him into the promised land.

Jesus also knows what it's like to spend time in the wilderness. Following his baptism by John, "At once the Spirit sent him out into the wilderness, and he was in the wilderness forty days, being tempted by Satan. He was with the wild animals, and angels attended him" (Mark 1:13).

God not only leads us into the wilderness and goes with us each step of the way. In his Son Jesus Christ, he lived there as well. Jesus experienced firsthand what it was like to trust God the Father in a desert place. He chose to live a holy life amid times of abundance and in the face of severe deprivation. Regardless of his circumstances, Jesus chose to live a holy life. Blessed be Yahweh M'Kaddesh!

CHAPTER 9

OF TEETER-TOTTERS AND CYCLES

(Yahweh Shalom)

PEACE IS HARD to come by in a war zone. Those of us who've spent time living with the fear of imminent injury or death in combat come up with many ways to alleviate its dreadful effects. For some, it was a preoccupation with work, tinkering about with electrical gadgets, music, or gambling. For others, it was alcohol or drugs. For me, it was a daily influx of my fiancé's letters. Her mail acted as a sedative. Each letter contained the medicinal ingredients needed to dispel the agitating effects of war. My daily medication of letters was a much-needed antidote. But, of course, it didn't last. I needed another daily fix to keep my fears under control.

Another way to alleviate the emotional toll of war was to send G.I.s on R&R—rest and relaxation. Once during a soldier's tour of duty, they could spend a week outside of Vietnam. Favorite spots included Hawaii or somewhere in Southeast Asia. I was able to travel to Sydney, Australia. Nice! It worked for a while, but then I had to get on a plane and fly back to Da Nang. I was again in war, and the fears returned. Not so nice!

The promised land proved to be something of a war zone. A new generation grew up in the wilderness and became more willing than their parents to enter the promised land by faith. Once in Canaan, they spent time

God's Gift of Intimacy

clearing the land of peoples who had lived a life of rebellion and unrepentant wickedness.

Unfortunately, faith is not a genetic marker. It can't be passed down from parent to child, like blue eyes and brown hair. One generation walks with God; the next walks away from him. Mothers and fathers may exhibit trust and devotion to the Lord. Sons and daughters: active rebellion or passive indifference.

It's like riding on a teeter-totter in the playground. At one point, you're up in the air, but then you dip down to the ground. Up and down, repeatedly. This is the way it was with the people of Israel. One generation followed God faithfully believing he would lead them to victory over their enemies. The next generation chose to rebel against God and suffered defeat.

Not only does one generation differ dramatically from another, but several generations also go through a repetitive cycle of rebellion and disaster followed by repentance and deliverance. The book of Judges catalogs several of these cycles. One such example involved a man by the name of Gideon. His generation was at the bottom ebb of the teeter-totter faith experience and in the middle of a cycle of rebellion and restoration.

The Book of Judges records this cycle (the fifth in a series): "The Israelites did evil in the eyes of the LORD, and for seven years he gave them into the hands of the Midianites" (Judges 6:1). We read that after suffering intense deprivation at the hands of their oppressors, "Midian so impoverished the Israelites that they cried out to the LORD for help" (6:6).

In response to their supplication, the LORD first sent them a prophet (unnamed) who reminded them of the rebellious acts they had committed (see 6:7–10). Then he raised up a man who would lead them into victory over the Midianites and help restore the people once again to God. That man was Gideon.

53

Gideon, however, had been as much impacted by this cycle as his fellow countrymen. He would need some convincing that the Lord had chosen him to be their leader and judge (see Judges 6:11–16).

To accomplish this, the angel of the LORD appeared to him and, through a sign, brought Gideon to the level of faith needed to trust God. This sign was so stupendous it almost backfired. As Gideon offered his visitor an offering of meat and unleavened bread, the angel of the LORD touched it with his staff, and fire suddenly erupted out of the rock that consumed the meat and bread (6:20–21). Surely that was enough to convince Gideon that he'd indeed been called to lead the people. But what the angel of the LORD did next provoked in Gideon a sense of dread and fear: "And the angel of the LORD disappeared. When Gideon realized that it was the angel of the LORD, he exclaimed, 'Alas, Sovereign LORD! I have seen the angel of the LORD face to face!'" (6:21–22).

What happened? God had sent a man (a prophet) to rehearse their rebellious acts. As a man, Gideon believed that God would use him to lead the revolt against the Midianites. Perhaps he thought that God had sent another man to convince him of this. But, when this strange visitor suddenly vanished out of his sight, he realized this wasn't a mere man. Instead, he was a being that may very well have been the LORD himself.[4] And he had seen him face to face. Not good!

Seeing my fiancé face to face after being gone for a year in Vietnam was a joyous experience. It was something I'd looked forward to for a long time. Why then would the thought of seeing God evoke such feelings of fear and anxiety for Gideon? What emotional triggers are at work here?

Once we take into consideration the emotional impact sin has in our lives, we can better understand Gideon's negative reaction upon encountering God so intimately. In the book of Genesis, we read that Adam and Eve were

---

4   To gain an understanding of the appearances of God in the Old Testament in general and the Angel of the Lord in particular, see J. C. Moyer's contribution entitled "Theophany," p. 1087 in *Evangelical Dictionary of Theology* edited by Walter A. Elwell.

free to eat the fruit from any tree in the garden except one. The prohibition came with a dire judgment: "You are free to eat from any tree in the garden; but you must not eat from the tree of the knowledge of good and evil, for when you eat from it you will certainly die" (Genesis 2:16--17). Suffering and death are the consequences of sin.

Sadly, Adam chose to disobey God and ate from the fruit of the forbidden tree. The result: "Then the man and his wife heard the sound of the LORD God as he was walking in the garden in the cool of the day, and they hid from the LORD God among the trees of the garden" (Genesis 3:8). Why did they hide? Adam's anxious response: "I heard you in the garden, and I was afraid because I was naked; so I hid" (Genesis 3:10).

Sin makes us fearful of being in the presence of a holy God, so we go into hiding. We instinctively seek to avoid God's presence out of fear of judgment for the sins we've committed. Sin triggered in Gideon the same kind of emotional response that we've all felt since our first parents disobeyed God in the garden.

To make matters worse, God had warned Moses: "You cannot see my face, for no one may see me and live" (Exodus 33:20). What seemed to be a blessing, Gideon interpreted as a death sentence. All the fear and dread of facing imminent death swept over him.

God created us to be in relationship with him, to enjoy his company and rejoice in his presence. This was almost certainly what Adam and Eve experienced before they chose to rebel against him. Notice that they were familiar with the sound of God walking in the garden. It was not this sound that evoked fear, but the reality of sin itself. Without sin, man's experience of God would be joyous and peaceful. But because of sin, it's anything but that.

To break the cycle of national disobedience and restore the people to himself, God first broke the cycle of sin and fear in Gideon's own life. He reassured him that the consequences for meeting God were not catastrophic as he thought. God told him, "Peace! Do not be afraid. You are not going to die" (Judges 6:23). Good news!

In response, Gideon, like Moses and Abraham before him, "Built an altar to the LORD there and called it The LORD Is Peace. To this day it stands in Ophrah of the Abiezrites" (Judges 6:24). The LORD is Peace is the meaning of the name Yahweh Shalom. God brings peace to troubled hearts.

Just as Gideon must have been relieved to hear the good news, we too can rejoice knowing that God has decisively dealt with sin in our lives. It is true that a holy God must punish sin, but He has lovingly and graciously provided His only begotten Son to be our sin bearer.

Isaiah wrote a theology of the cross centuries before Christ was crucified. Speaking prophetically, Isaiah said of God's Son,

> "Surely he took up our pain and bore our suffering,
> yet we considered him punished by God, stricken
> by him and afflicted. But he was pierced for our
> transgressions, he was crushed for our iniquities; the
> punishment that brought us peace was on him, and
> by his wounds we are healed" (Isaiah 53:4--5).

The "punishment that brought us peace" was borne by Jesus who died for our sins (see 1 Corinthians 15:3). As a result, "there is now no condemnation for those who are in Christ Jesus, because through Christ Jesus the law of the Spirit who gives life has set you free from the law of sin and death" (Romans 8:1--2). Christ's death has set us free from the condemnation that comes from a lifetime of sin.

Adam chose to rebel against God, and he suffered the consequences for his sin. Conversely, when we choose to put our faith in Christ's substitutionary death, we reap the consequences of God's grace:

> Therefore, since we have been justified through faith,
> we have peace with God through our Lord Jesus

Christ, through whom we have gained access by faith into this grace in which we now stand. And we boast in the hope of the glory of God" (Romans 5:1--2).

Peace rather than fear characterizes the emotional intimacy we share with God. Shalom!

CHAPTER 10

WHO'S IN YOUR FOX HOLE?
(Yahweh Sabaoth)

SOME OF THE scariest moments while flying missions in Vietnam came when something unexpected happened. On one mission, our helicopter cockpit was suddenly sprayed with pink colored liquid. We panicked thinking that a hydraulic line had burst. Fortunately, our crew chief discovered that the cap on his canteen had backed off, spewing strawberry Kool-Aid everywhere. On another flight, I discovered that I still had a round in the chamber of my machine gun. No big deal, I fired the round. As the casing ejected, it suddenly took a weird turn and bounced off the back of the copilot's helmet. Hearing the lone shot and feeling the hit from the casing caused the pilot to believe he'd been shot. He almost lost control of the helicopter in his panic.

On another occasion, while we were en route to our destination, the pilot spotted a person crouching in a foxhole…and he was armed! Assuming he was the enemy, we quickly swung back around and made our approach planning to eliminate him. The man suddenly realized the dire situation he was in. He jumped out of the foxhole, put his rifle down, and started waving his arms about, pointing at his camouflaged uniform. We all quickly recognized the distinctive pattern of his clothing and concluded he wasn't the enemy. Instead, he was a South Korean soldier (we called them Rock Marines). He was spared in just the nick of time.

It was quite remarkable to encounter a soldier alone in a foxhole with no fellow soldiers around him. He faced the enemy with no one to help him. I don't know if he was courageous or crazy. Maybe both. I only knew I was glad I wasn't him.

At times, we may be tempted to feel like that soldier. There's no one else in the foxhole to keep you company or to help you face your challenges. It's up to you, and you could be eliminated at any time.

A young shepherd boy by the name of David seemed to be in a similar predicament. He had been tending his father's sheep while three of his brothers were serving in the army. He travelled to the battle front to deliver much needed food supplies. Once there, he inquired how the war was going (see 1 Samuel 17:1–11).

What he learned was alarming. The army of Israel had drawn up in battle against their enemy the Philistines. But rather than fight, the Israelites were paralyzed with fear and were doing nothing. Why? The Philistines had challenged the Israelites to a one-on-one match between their champion warrior Goliath and anyone who was courageous (or crazy) enough to fight him. It was winner take all. Whoever wins, the other team (country) loses and becomes defeated servants.

Goliath's appearance was certainly impressive and menacing (1 Samuel 17:4–7). It was enough to keep everyone at bay. Everyone that is except David. Without hesitation, he determined to go mano a mano with the big guy. If you were there and stood David next to Goliath, you might have told David to stick with the catering business and leave the fighting to the professionals.

The contest between David and Goliath represented more than a smack down between two warriors and feuding armies. It was a conflict between two rival world views. On one side was Goliath who viewed reality through the lens of polytheism. To him, a multitude of gods, goddesses, and demons inhabited the universe. Each deity jockeyed for control of some aspect of

THE GREATEST PRESENCE OF ALL

the natural and social order. Respect for the local god of interest determined whether you were successful in life's endeavors.

As strong as Goliath was, he still relied on the favor of the gods. This was evident in his contemptuous outburst at seeing young David approaching him in battle: "He said to David, 'Am I a dog that you come at me with sticks?' And the Philistine cursed David by the gods" (1 Samuel 17:43).

David, on the other hand, viewed Goliath and the battle through the lens of monotheism. Following the exodus from Egypt, the Lord had been steering the people ever more closely to an understanding that only one God exists who is Lord over all creation. Moses rehearsed to the people the things that God had done to help them embrace this radically different world view. In the Torah (first five books of Moses) we read,

> Has any god ever tried to take for himself one nation
> out of another nation, by testings, by signs and wonders,
> by war, by a mighty hand and an outstretched arm,
> or by great and awesome deeds, like all the things
> the LORD your God did for you in Egypt before
> your very eyes? You were shown these things so
> that you might know that the LORD is God; besides
> him there is no other (Deuteronomy 4:34–35).

David's response to Goliath's diatribe revealed how much his monotheistic mindset had influenced him: "You come to me with sword, a spear, and a saber, but I come to you in the name of the LORD of armies, the God of the armies of Israel, whom you have defied" (1 Samuel 17:45, NASV). LORD of armies is the meaning of the name Yahweh Sabaoth. David not only believed Yahweh was the God of the army of Israel. He also declared God was Yahweh Sabaoth, the Lord over all armies in heaven and on earth.

From David's perspective, Goliath's reliance on his gods was futile. Only Yahweh Sabaoth existed to rule over the armies of the earth. And Goliath had defied him. Yikes!

60

God's Gift of Intimacy

Other than his armor bearer, Goliath stood alone on the battlefield. There were no gods there to lend him support—no thunderbolts, tridents, silver bows, or hefty hammers at his disposal. He was like that South Korean soldier who crawled out of his foxhole waving his arms about hoping to stave off a devastating strike from a fully loaded helicopter gunship.

Unlike Goliath, David wasn't alone. Yahweh Sabaoth was with him. His presence more than made up for David's physical shortcomings. As David confidently affirmed,

> "This day the LORD will deliver you into my hands,
> and I'll strike you down and cut off your head. This very
> day I will give the carcasses of the Philistine army to the
> birds and the wild animals, and the whole world will
> know that there is a God in Israel" (1 Samuel 17:46).

David's personal knowledge was intended to be common knowledge. His confidence was meant to give the army of Israel confidence as well. The formula for his victory was intended for all who follow the Lord. As David testified, "All those gathered here will know that it is not by sword or spear that the LORD saves; for the battle is the LORD's, and he will give all of you into our hands" (17:47).

Both men may have sincerely believed what they said was true. But who was right? Which of these world views was true? From a purely pragmatic standpoint, the last man standing had the correct perspective. Scripture says that when they engaged in battle, this happened:

> As the Philistine moved closer to attack him, David ran
> quickly toward the battle line to meet him. Reaching
> into his bag and taking out a stone, he slung it and
> struck the Philistine on the forehead. The stone sank
> into his forehead, and he fell facedown on the ground.
> So David triumphed over the Philistine with a sling
> and a stone; without a sword in his hand he struck

THE GREATEST PRESENCE OF ALL

down the Philistine and killed him. David ran and
stood over him. He took hold of the Philistine's sword
and drew it from the sheath. After he killed him, he
cut off his head with the sword (1 Samuel 17:48–51).

David was right! Goliath was dead. He should have quit while he was
ahead! Sorry, I couldn't resist that.

David's encounter with Goliath is just one of many instances in the Bible
where people received the courage to face overwhelming challenges. When
Moses died, God commissioned Joshua to take his place. Leading the people
across the Jordan river into the promised land would seem an overwhelming
challenge. God, however, told him just what he needed to hear. In the book
of Joshua we read,

"Be strong and very courageous. Be careful to obey
all the law my servant Moses gave you; do not turn
from it to the right or the left, that you may be
successful wherever you go…Have I not commanded
you? Be strong and courageous. Do not be afraid;
do not be discouraged, for the LORD your God will
be with you wherever you go" (Joshua 1:7, 9).

Joshua, like David, was not the Lone Ranger. God was with him every
step of the way. The same was true for Christ's disciples. Jesus commissioned
his disciples to "go and make disciples of all nations, baptizing them in the
name of the Father and of the Son and of the Holy Spirit, and teaching them to
obey everything I have commanded you" (Matthew 28:19). Facing the nations
like facing Goliath is scary, but Jesus knew what would make the difference:
"And surely I am with you always, to the very end of the age" (28:20).

The picture of the solitary Christian soldier huddling in a foxhole waiting
for the enemy to come by is far from what we see in Scripture. Instead, God
himself is in our midst. His very presence gives us the confidence of victory
and the courage we need to face our challenges. We can thank our God that
he is eternally Yahweh Sabaoth!

CHAPTER 11

THAT'S RIGHT!

(Yahweh Tsidkenu)

DAVID WOULD EVENTUALLY become the king of Israel, and following him would be a line of kings. A handful would do what was right before God, but the rest would become a basketful of deplorables who did what was evil in the sight of the Lord. Unfortunately, the unrighteous acts of these kings had disastrous results for the kingdom.

Each new king usually dashed the hopes of a righteous and prosperous kingdom. In time, hope itself was lost, and a fatalistic attitude took over. One more king—another generation of suffering and despair. At a particularly low ebb, God sent a prophet by the name of Jeremiah with a message of hope. Speaking through him, God said,

> "The days are coming," declares the LORD, "when I will raise up for David a righteous Branch, a King who will reign wisely and do what is just and right in the land. In his days Judah will be saved and Israel will live in safety. This is the name by which he will be called: The LORD Our Righteous Savior" (Jeremiah 23:5–6).

This passage calls a person yet to come The LORD Our Righteous Savior, which is the meaning of Yahweh Tsidkenu. Jeremiah lived at a time when people, especially those in positions of power, chose to do the wrong thing. This vicious cycle happened again and again. But just when hope of ever seeing a righteous king seemed lost, God delivered words of hope. One day someone will come and right all wrongs. He will rule wisely, and the people will benefit from his decisions. God promised this will happen, and he is Yahweh Tsidkenu. His words and actions are always right.

We're all tempted at one time or another to give up hope. The thought that things can improve is often sacrificed on the altar of present despair. I know what that feeling is like. I stopped believing that I would ever come home from Vietnam alive. But God stepped in and gave me renewed hope. It was not an illusion. Here I am decades later writing this as a testimony to God's faithfulness to his children.

Unlike us, God isn't bound by temporal parameters. He sees our predicament from an eternal perspective. This means that God is not only aware of the circumstances that assail us today, but he also sees into the future. He knows how things will eventually turn out. And good things await those who trust him. This isn't based on wishful thinking but the certainty of God's word: "And we know that in all things God works for the good of those who love him, who have been called according to his purpose" (Romans 8:28).

As our Creator, God knows what we need to live a full and prosperous life. We need laws to set forth what is permitted and what is prohibited. So, God gave us law books (Torah) that clearly set forth the boundaries for human flourishing. In a similar way, we need instructions on how to live wisely. Accordingly, God revealed to us wisdom books, such as Job, Ecclesiastes, and Proverbs. In Job, we explore the complexities of human suffering. In Ecclesiastes, we delve into the meaning and purpose of life.

It is particularly in Proverbs that we find hundreds of pithy statements aimed at the reader developing skill in the art of godly living (in Hebrew the word is called *hokmah*). These godly principles cover most areas of human experience and relationships such as parent/teen and husband/

wife relationships, friendship, dating, sexual purity, finances, work, giving, thought life, foolish and wise speech, drinking, gossiping, decision making, humility, and pride, gladness, and joy, etc. All in all, this book gives us an overview on how to make right decisions and live life to the full.

While these resources are valuable to achieve a life of obedience and righteousness, we need more. We were made to be in constant fellowship with our Creator. His presence fills the relational void in our lives. That is why God promised to send us a book and raise a person who, as King, would live a righteous life before us. All those who are a part of his kingdom will reap the benefits of his righteousness. The question is, who is this future king?

Fortunately, Jeremiah's prophecy doesn't stand alone. Other prophets used similar language to describe this future king. The metaphor of a "righteous branch" in Jeremiah is a "branch bearing fruit" in the book of Isaiah. Isaiah also looked forward to a future day when a person will come forward filled with God's Spirit:

> A shoot will come up from the stump of Jesse; from his roots a Branch will bear fruit. The Spirit of the LORD will rest on him—the Spirit of wisdom and of understanding, the Spirit of counsel and of might, the Spirit of the knowledge and fear of the LORD (Isaiah 11:1–2).

As in Jeremiah, Isaiah declared that this person would exercise judgment based solely upon righteousness:

> He will not judge by what he sees with his eyes, or decide by what he hears with his ears; but with righteousness he will judge the needy, with justice he will give decisions for the poor of the earth. He will strike the earth with the rod of his mouth; with the breath of his lips he will slay the wicked. Righteousness will be his belt and faithfulness the sash around his waist (Isaiah 11:3–5).

The one who would be both the righteous branch of David and the branch bearing fruit from Jesse would have to be a descendant of both men. According to the Book of Acts, Jesus is just such a person:

> After removing Saul, he made David their king. God
> testified concerning him: "I have found David son of Jesse,
> a man after my own heart; he will do everything I want
> him to do." From this man's descendants, God has brought
> to Israel the Savior Jesus as he promised (Acts 13:22–23).

The Spirit of the Lord came upon Jesus, the seed of David and Jesse, and he acted righteously on behalf of the poor (see Luke 4:18). The Apostle John prophesied about Jesus who would come to exercise righteous judgment on the earth (see Revelation 19:11–13). Most amazingly, we who put our trust in Jesus receive God's righteousness: "God made him who had no sin to be sin for us, so that in him we might become the righteousness of God" (2 Corinthians 5:21).

The branch metaphor expressed by both Jeremiah and Isaiah speaks to an indispensable organic union in nature. Only branches interconnected with the trunk of the tree flourish. Sever the branch from the trunk, and the branch dies. Jesus also drew on this metaphor when describing the union between himself and his followers. Speaking to his disciples, Jesus said, "I am the vine; you are the branches. If you remain in me and I in you, you will bear much fruit; apart from me you can do nothing" (John 15:5).

Union and communion with our Creator and Savior are not derivative. These do not derive significance from other sources such as law books and moral codes. Instead, our relationship to our Creator and thus to one another is a basic and fundamental design feature necessary for our existence. Take away this relationship and we die. Creating us in this way was the right thing for our Creator to do. It was a righteous act. Praise be to Yahweh Tsidkenu!

CHAPTER 12
AND THE NAME OF THE CITY IS....
(Yahweh Shammah)

THE UNFAITHFULNESS OF the people of Israel had reached a tipping point. So prolific and deep-seated was Israel's unfaithfulness that a brief period of restoration under godly leadership such as that of king Josiah (640–609 BC) wasn't enough. God allowed Nebuchadnezzar, King of the Babylonian Empire, to lay siege against Jerusalem (589–587 BC) and take the people into captivity. God used captivity to raise up a generation of people committed to Him.

Just as God ministered to the people in the wilderness, he continued to reveal Himself to them while in captivity. God sent three prophets to speak forth his word to these wayward people. Daniel was a young man God used to speak to the young aristocrats taken into captivity to the city of Babylon. There, they were groomed for life and service in the Babylonian culture. Jeremiah stayed behind and spoke to the remnant of people left in Jerusalem. Ezekiel was commissioned by God to minister to the bulk of the people who made up a large settlement camp by the Kebar River located some two hundred miles north of the city of Babylon.

The siege against Jerusalem destroyed most of the houses, the wall, and the temple. It reduced the city of peace to rubble. For the next seventy years of captivity (see Jeremiah 29:10), the thought of a once glorious city as the center of God's promised land faded to a distant memory. It was time for a new vision of God's plan for the city and its people.

After devoting several messages to the people to help them endure their time of captivity and become the people God intended them to be, Ezekiel focused his attention on this once great city. In the last eight chapters of his book, Ezekiel gave a futuristic description of a magnificent city far surpassing that of the original.

Ezekiel went to great lengths describing the new temple: its walls, gates, rooms, altar, the priests who would serve there, holy days, and offerings (See chapters 40–46). He then gave a description of the land and how it was to be divided among the tribes of Israel (see Ezekiel 47–48:29). He even went so far as to describe the measurements of the city and its gates (Ezekiel 48:30–35).

Ezekiel closed his prophecy by giving the city a new name. It would no longer be called Jerusalem. In the last verse we read, "And the name of the city from that time on will be: THE LORD IS THERE" (Ezekiel 48:35). The LORD is there is the meaning of the Hebrew name Yahweh Shammah.

What makes this city special and unique is that God dwells there. His presence makes all the difference in the world. Can you imagine a travel brochure extolling the virtues of this city? In bold letters, it would read: **GOD DWELLS HERE!** In this city, you can meet many interesting people, but nothing compares to the prospect of having a meeting with God himself!

The Apostle John brought the last book of the Bible to a close with an apocalyptic revelation of a new city that comes down from heaven (see Revelation 21). Though there are some differences between Ezekiel's and John's visions of this heavenly city, one thing remained constant: the presence of God. John tells us,

> "And I heard a loud voice from the throne saying, 'Look!
> God's dwelling place is now among the people, and he will

dwell with them. They will be his people, and God himself will be with them and be their God'" (Revelation 21:3).

The heavenly city represents God's commitment to be with us forever. He is not here for a brief visit only to return to his celestial home. He makes his home with us. God moves into our neighborhood. Where we live is where our heavenly Father lives. He is not a guest, a frequent traveler, or someone stopping by to spend the night on his way to a more important place. He's here to stay.

Consider the outcome of God's presence in our lives: "He will wipe every tear from their eyes. There will be no more death or mourning or crying or pain, for the old order of things has passed away" (Revelation 21:4). This city stands out for what isn't there. To begin with, there's no cemetery in this city. There's no need for this community to set apart a portion of land to take care of loved ones who have died. Death is no more. There are no hospitals, prisons, homeless shelters, crisis pregnancy or drug rehabilitation centers, orphanages, or assisted living communities. There's no need for the military, police, FBI, CIA, or NCIS. Doors and gates have no locks. People will not need health or life insurance.

In the absence of violence, there is safety. Without suffering, sorrow, and death, there is peace and joy. Fear is gone; love abounds. Without the ugliness and squalor of poverty, there is beauty. People will not long for something better; life here is glorious.

God's presence produces the perfect utopian society people long for. All the political and social strivings for a place where everyone is equally valued will be fully realized in this city. Protests and riots will become artifacts of a bygone age.

Deep inside each human soul is a longing for a place and a presence where humans can reach their fullest potential without fear that one day everything will be washed away. Gone forever is the haunting thought that

THE GREATEST PRESENCE OF ALL

this is just the calm before the storm. In this city, the good and perfect remain constant. As John continued,

> "They will see His face, and His name will be on their foreheads. There will be no more night. They will not need the light of a lamp or the light of the sun, for the Lord God will give them light. And they will reign forever and ever" (Revelation 22:4–5).

All of this is made possible because the Lord is present with us. Blessed be the name of Yahweh Shammah!

CHAPTER 13

IMMANUEL'S LAND

(Immanuel)

THE YEARS BETWEEN Malachi, the last prophet of Israel, and the Gospel of Matthew have been called the "400 Silent Years." During this time, God didn't send any prophets with new revelations. Suddenly, God broke radio silence. An angel appeared to shepherds with startling news: "Today in the town of David a Savior has been born to you; he is the Messiah, the Lord" (Luke 2:11). The heavens then opened with an unexpected supernatural outburst: "Suddenly a great company of the heavenly host appeared with the angel, praising God and saying, 'Glory to God in the highest heaven, and on earth peace to those on whom his favor rests'" (2:13–14).

The astonishing display of supernatural pyrotechnics was all about the birth of a child. The question is, who is this child and why is he so important? To answer this question, we must go back nine months and ninety miles north of Bethlehem to check in on a young woman who lived in a small town called Nazareth. Her name was Mary.

It seemed like any other day. Chores needed care. Household duties required attention. Mary was fully engaged in these mundane but necessary tasks oblivious to the fact that the countdown for the entrance of the Savior of the world had just struck zero.

An angel by the name of Gabriel entered Mary's house with life-changing news: "You will conceive and give birth to a son" (Luke 1:31). Gabriel had more to say about how important this person was, but just the fact that she would become pregnant sent shock waves through Mary. Although she was engaged to a man named Joseph, they were not yet married. Both were committed to sexual purity. "How will this be,' Mary asked, 'since I am a virgin?'" (Luke 1:34)

To ease her troubled mind, Gabriel explained to her the miraculous nature of her conception: "The Holy Spirit will come on you, and the power of the Most High will over-shadow you. So the holy one to be born will be called the Son of God" (Luke 1:35). In support of his miraculous news, the angel announced that her cousin Elizabeth who was beyond childbearing years was six months pregnant. All of this was sufficient and necessary for Mary to accept her role in this unfolding redemptive drama.

One down, one to go. Joseph wasn't in the house when the angel spoke to Mary. He found out indirectly that the woman he was engaged to was pregnant. In response, Joseph felt he had no other choice but to end their relationship. This would require a legal procedure as an engagement in this culture was contractual.

While Joseph was asleep, an angel came to him in a dream to enlighten him about the miraculous nature of Mary's conception. The angel told him, "Joseph son of David, do not be afraid to take Mary home as your wife, because what is conceived in her is from the Holy Spirit. She will give birth to a son..." (Matthew 1:20–21).

The angel's visit in Joseph's mindscape also helps us as readers of God's word to gain a deeper understanding of the purpose for this miraculous conception. Scripture tells us, "All this took place to fulfill what the Lord had said through the prophet: 'The virgin will conceive and give birth to a son, and they will call him Immanuel (which means 'God with us')" (Matthew 1:22–23).[5]

One of the reasons for this stupendous miracle was so that God could be with us. His presence in our lives has been the theme throughout the Old Testament. Each of the names of God given in the historical context of people's lives gave ample proof that God desires to be in a dynamic relationship with us. The New Testament brings this truth into the fullest light with the birth of Immanuel.

To what extent would God be willing to go to be with us? From this passage and those to follow, we see that he who eternally possessed a divine nature also took upon himself a human nature so that his presence could be experienced at a human level—one human to another.

While words cannot adequately convey all that was involved for God to take upon himself our human nature, some truths stand out at once. First, God didn't become a man simply because circumstances required it. That would reduce the miracle of divine conception to an ad hoc knee jerk response to human needs. Instead, God had planned from all eternity to become human. Thus, the miracle of conception resides within the will of God and not just human necessity.

Scripture is careful to exposit how events unfold according to God's eternal purposes. The birth of Immanuel is one example. The prophet Isaiah served the Lord between 740 and 680 BC. He predicted that a virgin would conceive and bear a son whose name would be Immanuel. Matthew declared the birth of Christ fulfilled this prophecy. Isaiah also stated that such events don't happen by chance but according to God's sovereign decree. Speaking again through Isaiah, God said, "I make known the end from the beginning,

---

5   There seems to be a discrepancy between Isaiah's prophecy about the birth of a child and its fulfillment in the birth of Christ. John MacArthur addresses this problem in his book, *The MacArthur New Testament Commentary*, Matthew 1–7 pp. 19–21.

THE GREATEST PRESENCE OF ALL

from ancient times, what is still to come. I say: 'My purpose will stand, and I will do all that I please'" (Isaiah 46:10).

Eyewitness testimony of Jesus's human nature abounds in Scripture. For instance, the Apostle John writing in his first epistle testified, "That which was from the beginning, which we have heard, which we have seen with our eyes, which we have looked at and our hands have touched—this we proclaim concerning the Word of Life" (1 John 1:1). Jesus's physical entrance into our time/space reality had a corresponding impact on his disciples' physical senses. They looked into his face, heard him speak, and held his hands. They walked together, ate together, and cried together. When he was beaten, he suffered. When his body was cut open, he bled. When he was crucified, he died.

To say that his physical presence was an illusion or parlor trick to convince the gullible is far from the truth. Thomas, one of the disciples, refused to believe his fellow disciples' report that they had seen Jesus alive from the dead. Rather than give in sight unseen, Thomas retorted, "Unless I see the nail marks in his hands and put my finger where the nails were, and put my hand into his side, I will not believe" (John 20:25). A week later, Jesus appeared to Thomas and offered to submit to his demands: "Put your finger here; see my hands. Reach out your hand and put it into my side. Stop doubting and believe" (20:27). Jesus's body could hold up to the most rigorous of physical investigations.

After listing his eyewitness credentials, the Apostle John stated the purpose for giving his testimony: "We proclaim to you what we have seen and heard, so that you also may have fellowship with us. And our fellowship is with the Father and with his Son, Jesus Christ" (1 John 1:3). The purpose of Christ's physical presence as Immanuel is to give us the confidence and desire to enter a deeper relationship with him and fellow believers.

Sin has ruptured the bond that was meant to exist between us and God. Without a divine remedy, we're doomed to live out our days isolated from our Creator and alone. But God in his unfailing love for us sent his only begotten Son into the world so that through his death we can be reconciled to Him and have the gift of eternal life. All this was done through Jesus who "became flesh and made his dwelling among us" (John 1:14). All praise and glory to Immanuel!

CHAPTER 14

TWO SIDES OF ONE COIN

(Savior/Jesus and Lord)

SOMETIMES, A ONE-SIDED coin can be worth a lot. When I was a student at college, I took summer jobs to pay the bills. One of my jobs involved driving a dump truck in the Rocky Mountains in Colorado. The company I worked for was clearing some land to put in utilities for a housing development. As we dug up the ground, some workers uncovered the dump site of an old mining camp. At lunchtime, some of the employees would sift through the soil to see what they could find. I was usually too tired to join them, but on one occasion I decided to walk through the area and see what I could turn up. I happened to see a round copper-colored disc sticking out of the dirt. As I picked it up, I noticed that one side was blank, but the other side had markings on it. Dusting it off, I saw the words "John London Post Trader FT Laramie W.T." etched around the edge of the disc. "In Goods 25 cents" was inscribed in the center.

    The men who had been sifting through the dirt lined up their day's finds on the hood of a truck to see who had made the best haul of the day. Although I didn't know at the time what I'd found, I believed it was valuable. To test my theory, I put the disc in my pocket and quickly scoured the area until I found an old broken bottle. I walked down and placed the bottle on the hood alongside the other treasures. The men saw my bottle and laughed. Then, I pulled out the disc, and everything went silent. The men huddled around taking a close look at what was in my hand. One man offered to give me a gold nugget on the spot in trade for my one-sided entry. I refused.

Sometime later, my wife and I took a trip to Fort Laramie to find out more about my discovery. (This was around 1973). In the museum, we noticed a few discs like mine on display. I asked the employee what these were. She told me they were Indian trade tokens used by the post traders when buying goods from the Native Americans. I saw a few 50- and 75-cent trade tokens. I asked why there was no 25-cent token, and she said no one had ever found one. I said that I had and pulled out the disc. Her eyes lit up, and she excitedly asked if I wanted to donate it to the museum. I declined. Later that day, a ranger looked me up and offered me money for the disc. Again, I said no. I'm looking at the disc as I type this manuscript.

One-sided coins (tokens) may have value in certain circumstances, but a one-sided view of God has little or no value in divine epistemology. God reveals himself by names that go together like the head and tail of a coin. One cannot be fully understood and valued without the other. The two names that follow accomplish this divinely appointed dual function.

Savior/Jesus

The angel who appeared in Joseph's dream to ease his conscience also said, "She will give birth to a son, and you are to give him the name Jesus, because he will save his people from their sins" (Matthew 1:21). The name Jesus is the English version of the Latin name *Isus*, which comes from the Greek *Iesous*. From Greek, the name makes its way back through Aramaic and finally to the Hebrew name *Yehoshua* or Joshua. The Hebrew meaning of the name means "Yahweh saves."

The very purpose for Christ being here is to deal decisively with the problem of sin. By doing so, Jesus became our Savior. He didn't come to save us from a difficult relationship, a lousy job, or overdue bills. He came to save us from the worst problem we could ever have—Sin!

Sin describes our active rebellion and passive indifference to God's will. Sin is the label God gave for Adam's rebellious act in the garden, and it includes all of us in rebellion against him from that day on. Paul spoke to this ugly truth in his letter to the believers at Rome. He said, "Therefore, just as sin entered the world through one man, and death through sin, and in this way death came to all people, because all sinned" (Romans 5:12).

That all have sinned is confirmed in both Scripture and human experience. The Bible tells us, "For all have sinned and fall short of the glory of God" (Romans 3:23). We don't always need a theologian or a judge at our side to explain the ramifications of our sinful ways. Our guilty conscience often does a good job of telling us that what we said was wrong and we deserve to be punished for what we have done.

We're powerless to save ourselves from the evil grip of sin. Without a Savior, we're doomed to a life of guilt and shame, isolation, and death. But God in his love and wisdom sent his only begotten Son to do what we could not: "You see, at just the right time, when we were still powerless, Christ died for the ungodly" (Romans 5:6). He paid the penalty for our sins, and in his death, we who put our trust in Him as our Savior receive the gift of everlasting life (see Romans 6:23; 1 Corinthians 15:3; Ephesians 2:4–8). That's good news! But there's another side to this multifaceted truth.

Lord

When the angel announced the news of Christ's birth to the shepherds, he told them that the child born on that very day was the Savior (*Soter* in Greek). Side one. He went on to say this Savior is the Lord (see Luke 2:11). The Greek word *Kurios* is essentially the same as the Hebrew name *Adonai*, both meaning Lord or master. Side two.

God's Gift of Intimacy

Perhaps a caveat is in order here. It can be argued that the use of the word Lord in reference to Jesus serves more as a title than a name. In this sense, "Lord" describes Jesus's position in relationship to the created order and to us. However, this designation is used so extensively throughout the New Testament that the title Lord and the name Jesus blend into the scriptural tapestry as a seamless whole.

When we address someone as lord, we recognize this person's authority over a given sphere of life. Someone can be addressed as lord over a household, family, business, or government. They're the boss; they're in charge. A sign of respect would be to place oneself under the authority of the one who holds the position as lord or master.

Jesus's life and death were a demonstration of his willingness to submit his will to that of his heavenly Father. His physical body was no exception. He willingly sacrificed his body on our behalf so that God's will may be accomplished. He said in Scripture, "Here I am, I have come to do your will….and by that will, we have been made holy through the sacrifice of the body of Jesus Christ once for all" (Hebrews 10:9–10). By submitting his body to the lordship of his Father, we have been immeasurably blessed.

The night before his death, Jesus prayed in the garden that there might be another way aside from death on a cross to save people from their sins. And yet, even at this critical moment, Jesus was submissive to the will of his Father. In agony, Jesus prayed, "My Father, if it is possible, may this cup be taken from me. Yet not as I will, but as you will" (Matthew 26:39).

Jesus recognized his Father as Lord over his life. We too are to recognize Jesus as Lord over our lives as well. As Lord, Jesus gave his disciples their marching orders. He said to them, "All authority in heaven and on earth has been given to me. Therefore go and make disciples of all nations" (Matthew 28:18-19). Our willing involvement in the spread of the Gospel is a demonstration of our recognition of Jesus's lordship.

THE GREATEST PRESENCE OF ALL

The lordship of Jesus is more than a means to an end; it's the focus of salvation. In fact, one can't say they're saved unless they confess that Jesus is Lord. As the Apostle Paul said, "If you declare with your mouth, 'Jesus is Lord,' and believe in your heart that God raised him from the dead, you will be saved" (Romans 10:9). Clearly, Jesus as both Savior and Lord are two sides of one redemptive truth.

As important as lordship is to our understanding of salvation, it does little to enhance our desire for intimacy with God. Quite the contrary. For many, lordship brings to the surface negative images, none very appealing. There's the image of a self-important prince astride a white horse riding though the village while servants bow before him as they grow his crops, press his grapes, shoot his game, and provide for his every need. Even worse is the vision of a North Korean dictator whose decisions are absolute and absolutely oppressive. Maybe we need a Lord, but nobody wants one.

Thankfully, Jesus's notion of lordship was countercultural and of inestimable value. At a time when the disciples were competing with one another to see who the top dog in the discipleship hierarchy was (see Matthew 20:20–24), Jesus set them straight on the correct purpose and function of lordship. He said to his disciples,

> "You know that the rulers of the Gentiles lord it over
> them, and their high officials exercise authority over
> them. Not so with you. Instead, whoever wants to become
> great among you must be your servant, and whoever
> wants to be first must be your slave—just as the Son of
> Man did not come to be served, but to serve, and to give
> his life as a ransom for many" (Matthew 20:25–28).

The lord in God's kingdom is not the Sheriff of Nottingham. Instead, he's a lowly servant sacrificing himself for the wellbeing of those under his authority. We should want to know someone like this who uses his authority to benefit us, not himself.

80

The fragrant aroma of self-abandonment draws us into the beauty of his presence. To confess that Jesus is Lord is not a slavish response to a tyrant but the expression of a grateful heart to someone with the power to love us.

CHAPTER 15

IRON MAN WITH A KIPPAH

(Messiah)

EVERYONE LOVES A hero—a man or woman endowed with wisdom and strength who possesses noble qualities. They're that rare breed that overcomes hardship to become illustrious warriors. With the enemy vanquished, the kingdom comes along with a movie trilogy, tee shirts, hats, action figures, etc. Sorry, I think I went a little too far.

Heroes have that magnetic power to draw us close to them. We gladly swear our allegiance, honor, and fortune and consider ourselves privileged to march alongside them. Every act of valor is memorialized. They become legends, famous characters for ages to come.

Such a person emerges from the Bible. He's called Messiah. The English word Christ comes from the Greek word *Christos*, which in turn is taken from the Hebrew word Messiah (also spelled *Masiah*). The word in Hebrew means Anointed: a person set aside from the mundane to accomplish God's will in a unique and life-transforming way. It's primarily the meaning of the word and not the term (Messiah) itself that appears throughout the Old Testament. A public ritual in which oil is poured on his head verifies his calling.

Specifically, the Messiah is consecrated unto God and empowered to conquer the nation that has oppressed God's people. Having delivered them

God's Gift of Intimacy

from evil, the Messiah establishes God's kingdom rule on earth. Thus, the promises God made to the people beginning with Abraham are fully realized under the leadership of this triumphant king.

Scripture tells us that the Messiah will be a descendant of King David. God, speaking through the prophet Nathan to David, said,

> "'The LORD declares to you that the LORD himself will establish a house for you: When your days are over and you rest with your ancestors, I will raise up your offspring to succeed you, your own flesh and blood, and I will establish his kingdom. He is the one who will build a house for my Name, and I will establish the throne of his kingdom forever'" (2 Samuel 7:11–13).

In addition to this passage, whole chapters in the Old Testament are devoted to the regal splendor of the coming Messiah (see Isaiah 9 and 11; also, Zechariah 9 and 12).

Fast forward to Gabriel's visit to Mary. Not only did he clarify the miraculous nature of her conception, he also identified Jesus as the regal descendant promised to David. Speaking about Jesus, Gabriel said, "The Lord God will give him the throne of his father David, and he will reign over Jacob's descendants forever; his kingdom will never end" (Luke 1:32–33).

Throughout his public ministry, Jesus spoke and acted in ways that established his messianic credentials. When John the Baptist was put in prison, he may have entertained some doubts about Jesus. Considering this, John sent his disciples to receive some words of assurance from Jesus (see Matthew 11:2–3). In response, Jesus said,

> "Go back and report to John what you hear and see: The blind receive sight, the lame walk, those who have leprosy are cleansed, the deaf hear, the dead are raised, and the good news is proclaimed to the poor" (11:4–5).

The miracles Jesus performed weren't random power bursts with no other purpose than to sensationalize his ministry. Rather, they conformed to the pattern of the Messiah and what he would do when he comes (See Isaiah 35:3–6).

We shouldn't be overly critical of John. In many ways, Jesus was an enigmatic figure to his own disciples as well. Just when they thought they had figured him out, he said or did something that ripped up the boundaries of the box they'd put him in. Luke describes one such event. When Jesus got into the boat with his disciples, he promptly went to sleep. Suddenly a storm struck, and his disciples feared for their lives. Upon waking Jesus, they expected him to join them in keeping the boat from sinking. Jesus, however, did something totally unexpected. Akin to scolding an unruly teenager, he commanded the wind and the sea to be still. And unlike the teenager, they obeyed (see Luke 8:22–24).

This caused the disciples to question Jesus's identity: "In fear and amazement they asked one another, 'Who is this? He commands even the winds and the water, and they obey him'" (Luke 8:25). The answer to this question has far-reaching implications. Is it possible that Jesus, who calmed the storm, can bring rest to your turbulent soul as well? If he can do one, he can do the other.

After spending about three years with his disciples, Jesus asked some probing questions concerning his identity. The first one: "Who do people say the Son of Man is?" (Matthew 16:13). Their answer: "Some say John the Baptist; others say Elijah; and still others, Jeremiah or one of the prophets" (16:14). All of these would be commendable choices from a cultural perspective, but they're so far from the mark.

Jesus then zeroed in on them: "'But what about you?' he asked. 'Who do you say I am?'" (16:15) There's no getting around this question. It must be faced and answered. I wonder what I would have said if I were in their sandals. What would your answer be?

Simon Peter, one of Jesus's disciples, piped up: "You are the Messiah, the Son of the living God" (16:16). Peter wasn't equating Jesus with the prophets (as Islam does) but with the promised Messiah. Where did this insight come from? Jesus declared, "Blessed are you, Simon son of Jonah, for this was not revealed to you by flesh and blood, but by my Father in heaven" (Matthew 16:17). Peter's insight into the identity of Jesus came straight from the top— the Father himself!

Scripture makes it clear that the Messiah couldn't be a man God used in a special way. Rather, Jesus is the eternal God, the Son who became man to fulfill his divinely appointed role as the Messiah. Messiahship and divine sonship constituted Peter's twofold confession. And Jesus gave him an A+ for his answer. Way to go, Peter!

Unfortunately, not all our thoughts rate a passing grade. Erroneous ideas about God and his perfect plans can result in a host of disturbing thoughts and feelings. If not addressed promptly, this cognitive and emotional dissonance can lead a soul to beat out of tune with the Lord's heart.

This is what happened to Jesus's followers. His disciples had imbibed a cultural expectation regarding the role of the Messiah. As the conquering king, he would lead a revolt that would end Roman rule over Israel. Once liberated from their oppressors, Jesus would establish his kingdom rule, and all would be as it should be. It would be a straight shot to the throne for the Messiah, nothing in between. But there was. It was a cross!

The crucifixion got in the way and wreaked havoc on their expectations. For example, on the third day following his death, Jesus appeared to two of his disciples and inquired into their depressed state (see Luke 24:13–18). Referring to Jesus, they said,

> "He was a prophet, powerful in word and deed before
> God and all the people. The chief priests and our rulers
> handed him over to be sentenced to death, and they

THE GREATEST PRESENCE OF ALL

crucified him; but we had hoped that he was the one
who was going to redeem Israel" (Luke 24:19–21).

Jesus went to work to correct their misconceptions and renew them to
a joyous and hope-filled relationship with himself. First, he used Scripture
to show them that the Messiah must suffer and die. Then he reassured them
that although the crucifixion ended sin's reign over their lives, the Messiah's
rule remained on course. To support this, he revealed his identity as the
risen Savior who will one day establish God's kingdom on earth (see Luke
24:25–31). Their communion with the risen Savior resulted in a deeper union
with their Messiah. Jesus repeated this formula for all his disciples (see Luke
24:36–49).

The leaders had another problem. It wasn't just that they too couldn't
reconcile the cross with the crown regarding Messiah's role. They refused to
equate divine sonship with Messiah's identity. It was their obstinate denial of
his divine sonship that led them to violence and the cross.

For instance, when Jesus healed an invalid and told him to pick up his
pallet and go home, the religious leaders persecuted him as a Sabbath breaker
(see John 5:8–16). In response, Jesus said, "My Father is always at his work to
this very day, and I too am working" (John 5:17). This ignited a firestorm: "For
this reason they tried all the more to kill him; not only was he breaking the
Sabbath, but he was even calling God his own Father, making himself equal
with God" (5:18). Jesus immediately went from Sabbath breaker deserving
of persecution to blasphemer deserving of death. This happened numerous
times (see John 8:58 and 10:31–33).

Either Jesus was who he claimed to be or, in their eyes, an unrepentant
blasphemer. Standing before the leaders on the night before his crucifixion,
he was given one last chance to deny his sonship and avoid the cross. Failing
to expose him as a fraud via defective witnesses, the High Priest said to Jesus,
"I charge you under oath by the living God: Tell us if you are the Messiah, the
Son of God" (Matthew 26:63).

God's Gift of Intimacy

Just as Peter denied knowing Jesus to save his own life, Jesus could deny his sonship and escape crucifixion. Fortunately, Jesus didn't give into such pressure tactics: "You have said so" (Matthew 26:64) was his reply. To make sure the high priest wouldn't change his mind, Jesus continued: "But I say to all of you: From now on you will see the Son of Man sitting at the right hand of the Mighty One and coming on the clouds of heaven" (26:64). Jesus's quote from the prophet Daniel was by Jesus's day heralded as a Messianic prophecy (see Daniel 7:13).

That was all it took. The high priest went ballistic and said, "'He has spoken blasphemy! Why do we need any more witnesses? Look, now you have heard the blasphemy. What do you think? 'He is worthy of death,' they answered" (Matthew 26:65–66).

By refusing to acknowledge divine sonship, the leaders had alienated themselves from the promised Messiah. To rectify this, God sent them someone who was once one of them—Paul!

Paul's brief autobiography in Acts 22 and 23 (see also Galatians 1 and 2) reveals how uniquely positioned he was to witness to the Jewish leadership. Speaking to the Jews in Jerusalem who mistakenly thought he had desecrated the temple and taught against the law, he said,

> "I am a Jew, born in Tarsus of Cilicia, but brought up in
> this city. I studied under Gamaliel and was thoroughly
> trained in the law of our ancestors. I was just as zealous
> for God as any of you are today. I persecuted the followers
> of this Way to their death, arresting both men and
> women and throwing them into prison" (Acts 22:3–4).

Paul could identify with their world view as he was trained to view Scripture from a shared perspective. He also shared their zeal for God and was, like them, willing to persecute and punish anyone who posed a threat to their religious convictions.

THE GREATEST PRESENCE OF ALL

Later, when the Sanhedrin interrogated him, Paul declared, "My brothers, I am a Pharisee, descended from Pharisees. I stand on trial because of the hope of the resurrection of the dead" (Acts 23:6). By declaring himself a Pharisee, he had aligned himself with the most conservative and religious element within the Sanhedrin, the supreme court presiding over the Hebrew people (with Rome's permission, of course).

Following his dramatic conversion to Christ on the road to Damascus (see Acts 9:1–19), Paul's worldview did a 180. We read that instead of persecuting Christians upon entering Damascus, "At once he began to preach in the synagogues that Jesus is the Son of God" (Acts 9:20). His method for persuading the Jewish people about the true nature and saving work of the Messiah remained constant wherever he went. For example, while In Thessalonica,

> As was his custom, Paul went into the synagogue, and
> on three Sabbath days he reasoned with them from the
> Scriptures, explaining and proving that the Messiah
> had to suffer and rise from the dead. "This Jesus I am
> proclaiming to you is the Messiah," he said (Acts 17:2–3).

God finds a way to help us overcome obstacles that keep us from entering into fellowship with him. Regarding the Jewish people in general and leadership in particular, Paul took time to show them how their world view wasn't compatible with Scripture. He went from passage to passage to construct a biblical view of Christ's identity.

God is thorough. He sent Jesus once and for all to pay the penalty for our sins and pave the way for him to rule victoriously as Messiah. But he also continues to clear the way for him to rule over our lives today. We do indeed have a hero in Christ the Lord!

CHAPTER 16

I WOULD LIKE TO SPEAK WITH THE PERSON IN CHARGE

(God)

HAVE YOU EVER had a problem with your cell phone, computer, or internet and have called customer service only to get a recorded message like this? "You are caller number 45, and your wait time is approximately two hours and thirty minutes. Please stay on the line and maybe you'll get lucky." Or "If you'd like to speak to one of our troubleshooters, press one. If you can't reach a troubleshooter and your head is about to explode, press two."

Speaking to a live person may be just as frustrating. I was talking to a representative on the phone who it turned out wasn't an employee of the company I was trying to reach. Instead, they were an employee of a call center the company contracted. Perhaps the most frustrating experience is to speak to someone you can't understand or who asks for a detailed explanation of the problem. If I knew exactly what was wrong, chances are I could also fix the problem. All I could say (about ten times in as many ways) is that I turned the blasted thing on, and it doesn't work! EEEGADS!!!

Wouldn't it be wonderful if just once you could call and the person who answers is the company's owner and CEO? Just a brief explanation would be enough for them to know exactly what the problem is and how to fix it.

THE GREATEST PRESENCE OF ALL

Everything taken care of with just one call. Yay!!! That's what happens when you reach the person in charge.

In a similar yet more profound way, wouldn't it be great to be in touch with the person who knows exactly why you feel alienated from God and alone in this world? Not only would this person know what the problem is, but they'd also know how to restore your relationship with your Creator so it lasts forever. There is such a person. His name is Jesus.

Only God knows the deepest secrets of your heart and the problems that exist between you and Himself. That's why you need to come to Jesus—He is God! But does the Bible reveal this or are we reading into Scripture something that doesn't exist in reality?

Multiple layers of attestation in Scripture witness the inescapable truth that Jesus Christ, our Lord and Savior, is God. To begin with, it ascribes divine names to Jesus. The Apostle John spoke of Jesus as the Word who existed eternally as God prior to the incarnation: "In the beginning was the Word, and the Word was with God, and the Word was God" (John 1:1). From the very beginning of creation, Jesus existed with and as God (see Genesis 1:1).

The English word God is translated from the Greek name *Theos*. Both have essentially the same meaning. They refer to a person who is the divine being. Addressing someone by this name means that you're ascribing deity to this person. The Bible does exactly that in reference to Jesus.

Not only did John choose the word Theos to identify who Jesus essentially is, he also used the word *Logos*, translated "Word," to describe his divine attributes. To the Greek mind, Logos was the mind, the reason of God himself that controlled and gave order to all creation. But this was not some vague understanding of an impersonal philosophical absolute permeating all things. Concerning the word Logos as used by the Apostle John, Earl F. Palmer aptly said,

> "John's hymn presents the logos as personal. This is the force of the pronoun translated 'through him.'

90

God's Gift of Intimacy

> The logos is not a status of reality, as in Buddhist
> religious thought about ultimacy, or a divine
> impersonal power, as in current religious power and
> actualization movements. The logos is Person."[6]

Jesus is not the "force" in *Star Wars*. He is the Person who made the stars!

At the incarnation, Jesus, the divine being, also became a human being: "The Word became flesh and made his dwelling among us. We have seen his glory, the glory of the one and only Son, who came from the Father, full of grace and truth" (John 1:14). At the moment of conception, Jesus, who is God, also became man. Paul testified that a search of Jesus's human ancestry also reveals his deity. Concerning the people of Israel, Paul said, "Theirs are the patriarchs, and from them is traced the human ancestry of the Messiah, who is God over all, forever praised" (Romans 9:5)!

The Greek philosophers liked to say that all humans possessed a spark of divinity. In their minds, Jesus, like all men, shared some portion of the divine nature, even if it was but a tiny spark. The Bible, however, doesn't apportion out the divine nature this way. The whole not the part of God dwells in Jesus. "For in Christ all the fullness of the Deity lives in bodily form" (Colossians 2:9).[7]

Jesus's deity and humanity remained constant. When Thomas beheld the resurrected body of Jesus, he confessed, "My Lord and my God!" (John 20:28). As Christians, we wait for the glorious return of Jesus from heaven to establish his Messianic kingdom. When he appears, Paul tells us we will see, "the appearing of the glory of our great God and Savior, Jesus Christ" (Titus 2:13).

Many other passages testify that Jesus is the image of the invisible God made flesh (see 2 Corinthians 4:4; Colossians 1:15, and Hebrews 1:3). He is

---

6   Earl F. Palmer, *The Intimate Gospel* (Waco, Texas: Word Books, 1978), p. 18.

7   The assertion that Jesus is both fully man and God is hard to reconcile intellectually. See appendix C for an explanation of this and other "antinomies" found in the Bible.

both our Savior and our God (see 2 Peter 1:1). Jesus is not an apparition or some less-than-real manifestation of God, but as John stated in his epistle, "He is the true God and eternal life" (1 John 5:20).

Jesus's words and deeds matched his divine names and titles. He exercised divine prerogatives; he forgave sins, raised the dead and exercised judgment (see Mark 2:5–7, Luke 7:47–50, and John 5:21–23). He possessed divine attributes: he is omniscient and omnipotent, eternal, and immutable (see John 2:24–25, 4:28, 8:58, 21:17; 1 Corinthians 1:24, Hebrews 13:8). He is the Creator (see John 1:3, Colossians 1:16, and Hebrews 1:10). When he taught, Jesus claimed the same authority as God (see Matthew 7:24–29).

Jesus performed miracles only God could do. By turning water into wine and walking on water, he demonstrated power over the elements and superseded the laws of nature (see John 2:1–11 and 16:24). By immediately withering an olive tree, feeding 5,000 people, and healing a woman who was subject to bleeding for a dozen years, he revealed his ability to work free from the restraints of time (see Matthew 9:19–22, 21:18–20; and Mark 6:34–44). And by raising the dead, Jesus exercised power to reverse the very process of life and death at work in all of us.

John later wrote the book of Revelation in which he recorded many visions of the future leading up to the return of Jesus as the conquering hero (see Revelation 19:11–16). He was apparently so overwhelmed by what he saw that he mistakenly worshipped the angel who spoke to him in one of these visons. The angel quickly corrected him: "Don't do that! I am a fellow servant with you and with your fellow prophets and with all who keep the words of this scroll. Worship God!" (Revelation 22:9). Jesus, however, received worship for the very reason stipulated by the angel—He is God! The wise men, those who were healed, his disciples, the people in the city and the temple worshipped Jesus. (See Matthew 2:2, 11, 8:2, 14:33 21:14–16, 28:17; John 9:38.)

Someone may respond to all of this by saying that people are inherently biased in their opinions. A person from a different faith or no faith at all may look at this evidence and come to a different conclusion. Since we are limited by our own perspectives, we cannot say with certainty which view is the right one. Right?

Fortunately, we aren't left with only a human perspective. God the Father has weighed in on this matter and rendered his verdict as to whether his Son is God or not. In the book of Hebrews, the inspired author cited several passages in the Bible to prove that Jesus is superior to the angels (see Hebrews chapter one). One of the proofs of his supremacy was taken from Psalm 45:6,7. In contrast to the angels, we read,

> But about the Son he says, "Your throne, O God,
> will last for ever and ever; a scepter of justice will
> be the scepter of your kingdom. You have loved
> righteousness and hated wickedness; therefore God,
> your God, has set you above your companions by
> anointing you with the oil of joy" (Hebrews 1:8–9).

In the above passage, God the Father is speaking to His Son. Twice, he addresses him as "God." If the Father is God, then the Son must also be God, as the Father addressed the Son in the same way he referred to himself. Furthermore, the Hebrew name used in Psalm 45:6,7 for both the Father and the Son is Elohim. If God the Father didn't hesitate to address His Son as God, then we should have confidence to do the same.

Jesus knows something about all of us simply because he became one of us. He knows what human beings go through. He's aware of our feelings and struggles, our strengths, and limitations. This knowledge extends to all who have entered the vast stream of humanity.

But as God, Jesus knows you personally in a way no other human can. He knows your deepest secrets, ambitions, and desires. He knows everything we've ever said and done and the motives behind each. His knowledge of us is constant and complete. He has known us before we were born (see Jeremiah 1:4–5) and while we were being formed in our mother's womb

(Psalm 139:13–16). Even before we utter a word, he knows exactly what we're going to say (Psalm 139:1–6). No one is a stranger to Jesus. At once, he knows the thoughts and intents of the hearts of every person who has ever lived (John 2:24–25).

Jesus didn't reveal his divine knowledge and power just to show off his supernatural abilities. He doesn't use his divine attributes as a blunt instrument to beat us down and drive us away from him. Quite the contrary. While on earth, when he displayed his divine nature, it was to draw us near to himself.

When he spoke to the Samaritan woman at the well and revealed her personal background, it wasn't to expose her sinful past and make her feel ashamed. Instead, she put down her water pot, rushed back into the city, and said, "Come, see a man who told me everything I ever did" (John 4:29). The end result: "Many of the Samaritans from that town believed in him because of the woman's testimony, 'He told me everything I ever did'" (John 4:39).

On the night before his crucifixion, Jesus said that all his disciples would fail the basic test of discipleship. Peter, not wanting to be counted as one of them, denied what Jesus said (see Mathew 26:31–35). Maybe Jesus was mistaken. Perhaps he didn't know Peter as well as he thought he did. Nope! When the rubber met the road and Peter was confronted about his relationship with Jesus, he bit the dust not once but three times just as Jesus said he would.

How did Peter feel about his colossal failure? Scripture says, "And he went outside and wept bitterly" (Matthew 26:75). It's hard to come back from suffering such a crushing blow. By all accounts, Peter was washed up. Jesus had every right to be rid of him once and for all. But again, instead of driving Peter away, he did the opposite.

After his resurrection, Jesus appeared again to his disciples on the beach with fish and chips ready for breakfast. After they finished eating, Jesus focused his attention on Peter. He asked him three probing questions to correspond with each of Peter's three denials. They were all essentially the same:

God's Gift of Intimacy

"Do you love me?" (See John 21:15–17.) Each time, Peter attempted to answer the best he could (considering his recent denials) that he did love Jesus.

Each question must have felt like a knife sinking deeper and deeper into Peter's soul. Finally, Peter burst out, "Lord, you know all things; you know that I love you" (John 21:17). Peter could no longer appeal to his inner strength, determination, or resolve. Instead, he threw himself upon the knowledge of God to confirm what his words couldn't convey.

What Jesus did to Peter wasn't an act of cruelty. Jesus had just performed open heart surgery. Peter suffered a broken heart by trusting in what he thought he knew about himself. He was wrong. His knowledge was faulty. Now, Jesus helped Peter acknowledge and depend upon Jesus's divine knowledge so that in the future Peter might successfully navigate the challenges of discipleship. With surgery complete, Jesus said to Peter, "Feed my sheep" (John 21:17). The fisherman became a shepherd!

After looking at the evidence myself and considering all that Jesus has done in my life, I bow my knee before Jesus and confess as Thomas and so many others have done, "My Lord and my God!"

CHAPTER 17

PAID IN FULL AND ON TIME!

(Redeemer)

WHEN MY TWIN brother and I graduated from high school, we thought we were finally free. We no longer had to get up each morning and get ready for school. We didn't have to follow a daily routine going from one boring class to another. Faculty and staff didn't have the authority to tell us what to do, how to think, or what to wear. We could come and go as we liked. We were free to do whatever we wanted.

We packed as much fun and freedom as we could into the summer of our graduation. But as summer came to an end and many of our friends packed up and went to college or work, we didn't want to do either. Finally, we decided as well—we joined the Marine Corps!

In the Corps, we soon realized we were no longer free to come and go as we chose. Having signed up for four years of active duty, we had placed ourselves under a higher authority. We had to obey orders or suffer the consequences. We quickly learned we couldn't be in the Marine Corps and do whatever we wanted too.

The grand illusion of sin is to think that the purpose of existence is to live a life free from a higher authority. We resist any thought of living a surrendered life in obedience to the will of another. Instead, we strive for self-autonomy—to be the master of our own domain, the captain of the ship. We want to call the shots, determine our own destiny, be our own god. That is exactly what sin is all about. The more we declare our own self will, the more we swear allegiance to sin.

What we fail to realize is that the true gift of life is to exercise our free will by placing ourselves under the authority and lordship of our Creator. When we rebel and choose to follow our own way, we are in fact placing ourselves under the authority and rule of sin. The autonomous life is, in reality, a life lived in obedience to sin.

This was the problem for the believers in Rome. They suffered from a misunderstanding about how to live a life once saved from sin. They apparently thought freedom from sin meant they were free to either continue to sin without consequence or live a life of righteousness without obligation. Wrong! The Apostle Paul stated,

> "Shall we sin because we are not under the law but under grace? By no means! Don't you know that when you offer yourselves to someone as obedient slaves, you are slaves to the one you obey—whether you are slaves to sin which leads to death, or to obedience, which leads to righteousness?" (Romans 6:15–16).

The manifold problem regarding sin is not only that we're guilty before a holy God for our sins (see Romans 3:19, 23), but we fail to see that freedom from sin's guilt and condemnation doesn't give us the freedom to sin without enslavement. We are free to place ourselves under the authority of Christ and no other. And there is a price to be paid to release a person from captivity to sin.

We've come a long way from the time people were bought and sold on the slave market. But in Paul's day, slave markets were part and parcel of life in the Roman Empire and beyond. It wasn't unusual to pay a price to free someone from slavery. The price varied according to the age, ability, education, and

THE GREATEST PRESENCE OF ALL

health of the individual. It also hinged on the wealth and position of the one making the payment. The slave dealer might raise the price if he thought the buyer had the ability and desire to pay more.

In a similar way, there's a price to be paid for sinners to be set free from enslavement to sin. Unlike traditional slave markets, the purchase price is based entirely upon the buyer's ability and desire to set the captives free. The most prized possession the buyer has is the purchase price for sinners. And in this case, the purchase price was the death of God's only begotten Son.

As a parent, I may be willing to give up my savings, surrender the title to my car, or give away my belongings if it means someone I love could be set free from the slave market. But I confess, giving up any of my children for another would be sheer agony. My love for my family fills the deepest recesses of my being.

Our heavenly Father loved us so much that he was willing to give up his only begotten Son so that we might be set free from the slave market to sin. John 3:16 is perhaps one of the most familiar verses in all of Scripture for a reason. It declares the extent God went to set us free: "For God so loved the world that he gave his one and only Son, that whoever believes in him shall not perish but have eternal life."

Jesus took upon himself the role of Redeemer: He paid the ransom price required to set captives free. The Apostle Peter declared,

> "For you know that it was not with perishable things
> such as silver or gold that you were redeemed from
> the empty way of life handed down to you from your
> ancestors, but with the precious blood of Christ, a
> lamb without blemish or defect" (1 Peter 1:18–19).

The blood of Christ himself was the ransom required, but when was the price to be paid? Paul wrote to the believers in the Province of Galatia, "But when the set time had fully come, God sent his Son, born of a woman, born

98

under the law, to redeem those under the law, that we might receive adoption to sonship" (Galatians 4:4)

God had marked off a propitious moment in time by which to send forth his Son into our time and space. The prophecies of Scripture aligned themselves perfectly with the movement of history to form a unique moment in time in which Christ came as our redeemer.

God didn't hesitate to send his Son. He wasn't one minute late. He was right on time. His timing, coupled with the purchase price paid, tells us how much God loves us and desires to be with us. The convergence of time and space with Christ our redeemer provides a level of intimacy unparalleled in human history. Christ forever lives as our Redeemer!

Loneliness demands time to consume us. It seeps into our days, weeks, and months, and rules over the calendar of life's activities. We end up too preoccupied with emptiness to embrace intimacy. But God's love for us penetrates the deepest recesses of our being. His desire for us triggers within us a corresponding desire to be loved.

One purpose for enumerating the names and titles of God has been to reassure those who are already redeemed, who have put their trust in Christ as Savior and Lord, that they possess an eternal, unbreakable relationship with their Creator (see 1 John 5:13). This assurance was woefully lacking at the beginning of my walk with the Lord. But for those who have yet to make a decision of faith, hopefully, the convergence of God's names with our human needs has created a deep longing to receive his forgiveness and enter into a personal relationship with Him.

Just as God has provided a time for Christ to redeem us from our sins, he has also provided a time for us to respond to his gracious provision. The Apostle Paul declared to the Corinthians, "I tell you, now is the time of God's favor, now is the day of salvation" (2 Corinthians 6:2).

If this is your time, you can respond with a simple prayer of confession and reception. By prayer, acknowledge that as a sinner, you are separated from God and cannot experience his abiding love. You also recognize that Christ has paid the full penalty for your sins and that it is your desire to receive him as your Savior and Lord. Perhaps there is no better time than right now to express your heart's desire to God in prayer.

CHAPTER 18

"IT'S JESUS...IT'S IN HIM!"

(Alpha and Omega)

YEARS AGO, A commercial came out featuring a young man stirring a pot of spaghetti. His father, seeing the empty jar next to the pot, was not impressed. As the self-appointed connoisseur of Italian cuisine, he began to rattle off ingredients that make for an acceptable sauce. In reply, the son assured the father, "It's Prego...It's in there." Finally, the father did a taste test to which he agreed, "It's in there!" I guess the commercial worked, as the product is still on the market today.

In the closing chapter of the Bible, the Lord Jesus said, "Look, I am coming soon! My reward is with me, and I will give to each person according to what they have done. I am the Alpha and Omega, the First and the Last, the Beginning and the End" (Revelation 22:12–13). The words Alpha and Omega refer to the first and last letters of the Greek alphabet, the original language of the Book of Revelation.

Jesus was present at the beginning of all that was created and revealed by God. He will also be present at the culmination of history and the final revelation of God's glory. Jesus's life serves as living bookends to all that encompasses God's creative and redemptive acts in time and space. He is the eternal "I Am," and all things find their ultimate fulfillment in him.

The comprehensiveness of Alpha and Omega cannot be overstated. In Jesus, the ABCs of God's grace are clearly spelled out. It is in and through him that the language of divine love is clearly read; not one chapter is missing. He completes in himself all that the Psalms, Writings, and Prophets, as well as the Apostles spoke about. Through him, the full spectrum of divine revelation emanates. Jesus is both the light and the life of the world. All that is directly stated or implied regarding God's desire to have union with us is assumed in the name Alpha and Omega.

There are many more names and titles of God that are not mentioned in this book. For example, God is *El Chay* – The Living God, *El Deah* – The God of Knowledge, *El Gibbor* – The Mighty God, *Yahweh Bore* – The Lord Creator, and *Yahweh Tsuri* – The Lord Our Rock. He also reveals himself as *El Chuwl* – The God Who Gave You Birth, and Abba – Father. Jesus is also called The Amen, The Almighty, Author of Life, Chief Shepherd, and Deliverer. And there are many more that can be covered. In fact, some lists of divine names and titles found in Scripture extend well into the hundreds.

Considering there are so many names and titles, I've chosen to be selective in the ones I've written about. I plead the name Alpha and Omega as an umbrella title to cover all the many more names directly stated or alluded to in the Bible I haven't covered.

In my defense, the Apostle John was also selective in writing about the signs and wonders Jesus performed (see John 20:30–31). Indeed, it would be practically impossible to give an exhaustive account of all that Jesus said and did while he dwelt among us (see John 21:25). Luke, the assumed author of the Book of Acts, gave only a summary account of the many appearances of Jesus to his disciples following his resurrection. And there were many more teachings Jesus and his Apostles gave that the Bible didn't include.

What then are the necessary ingredients that go into making the most intimate relationship between God and humanity? Surely, love must be the number one ingredient. Grace, mercy, and kindness sweeten the relationship as well. No union would be complete without generous servings of faith and hope well-seasoned with joy. Be sure to add a pinch of patience while you're at it. We would respond to all the self-appointed connoisseurs of human/divine relationships, "Its Jesus...It's in Him!" He is the Alpha and Omega.

CHAPTER 19

A TALE OF TWO PRAYERS

I BEGAN THIS book with two stories. The first was about how God revealed himself to me in ways that changed my life forever. I intended the second to show that God made this same difference in a nation of people. His presence has not only changed their lives but the course of history as well.

It seems appropriate now to end this book with two prayers. The first is your personal prayer. The second is the Lord's Prayer given the night before he was crucified. Each prayer highlights common themes, namely that the Lord changes our lives and those of all who follow Jesus.

Your Prayer

As we've seen, God revealed his names and titles in context with the needs of the people he loves. When they called upon God by one of his many names, they recognized his desire to be with them and that his presence makes a difference in their lives. By way of personal application, you're invited to craft a prayer that aligns the names of God with your own personal circumstances.

Perhaps a sample prayer will be helpful. Consider this: Sally is suffering from low self-esteem. Billy's mother is ill. Mike likes the idea of God but refuses to submit to him. Becky feels like she's invisible; nobody sees and understands what she's going through. Mary is insecure about life. She feels that if she had more money, a better career, or new friends she would experience a sense of fulfillment. John is constantly anxious; he desperately needs to relax, but his mind is overwhelmed with issues. Amanda isn't saved and is struggling with guilt and shame. The following prayer is a sample of how the names and titles of God can relate to each of these persons.

"Elohim, I pray for Sally. Help her to understand that she was created in your image and has inestimable value. May she experience the majesty of your presence in her life. Yahweh Rapha, I lift up to you Billy's mother. As you have healed others with many afflictions, I pray that if it is your will, you may heal her as well. Sovereign Kurios and Adonai, help Mike to see that submission to your will is the path to an abundant and joyous life. El Roi, I pray for Becky. Help her to understand and rejoice that you see her, and you do understand what she's going through. I ask that you open the eyes of her soul to see your glorious presence in her life. Gracious El Shaddai, I pray for Mary. I pray she will experience the all-sufficiency of your presence in her life. Help her to find fulfillment and satisfaction that comes from an abiding relationship with you. Yahweh Shalom, I pray for John that he may experience your peace in his life. May he rest in your presence and experience calmness of mind and soul. Jesus, I pray for Amanda that she may come to you and find salvation from her sins. May she experience forgiveness and freedom from guilt and shame. I pray these things knowing that you are Yahweh Yireh. You alone can provide what we need most in our lives. I ask these things in the name of Jesus Christ our Lord. Amen."

Now it's your turn. Would you take some time to list some of your deepest concerns. Then, match one of God's names or titles to your needs. Making sure that your prayer is well seasoned with thanksgiving, present your requests before God (see Philippians 4:6). I have a hunch that a prayer such as this will expand your experience of his grace and bring you peace.

The Lord's Prayer

Could it be that the promised kingdom was about to be established? Jesus had just made his triumphal entry into Jerusalem. The crowds cheered him and waved palm branches, the symbol of Jewish nationalism. They shouted out, "Hosanna! Blessed is he who comes in the name of the Lord! Blessed is the king of Israel!" (John 12:13). "Hosanna," which means "Save now," suggested that the people expected the revolution was about to begin. They recognized that Jesus was indeed sent to them by no less than the Lord himself. They declared him to be the king of Israel. It was all coming together.

Jesus's disciples must have trembled with anticipation at the thought that after three years following him, their investment was about to pay off. This may explain why they once again squabbled over who got the highest seats of honor in the Lord's kingdom (See Luke 22:24–30).

Once he entered the city, Jesus met privately with his disciples in an upper room of a private home. Maybe now Jesus would reveal the plan of action that would ignite a revolution first in Jerusalem and then spread throughout Israel. At last, they would be free from the cruel tyranny of Rome! What Jesus said to them was indeed explosive, but not in the way they expected. He told them he was leaving them! What!!!

Jesus, fully aware of God's perfect plan, knew that "the hour had come for him to leave this world and go to the Father" (John 13:1). It was not time for him to ascend to the throne, but to depart.

Sometimes it hurts to admit our understanding isn't on the same page of God's storybook. This is one case in point: The disciples were running on a plan of their own making. Surely, as the Messiah, Jesus should do this and that according to their expectations. They failed to understand that God's plan was far more comprehensive than theirs.

Jesus knew that the work of saving sinners was ending. The final actions that would lead to his crucifixion and death were about to commence.

Therefore, Jesus said to the Father, "I have brought you glory on earth by finishing the work you gave me to do" (John 17:4). Mission accomplished! Jesus, who came from God the Father, was now returning home: "I came from the Father and entered the world; now I am leaving the world and going back to the Father" (John 16:28). All of this may be true, but absolutely devastating for his disciples.

How hard it must've been for the disciples to hear Jesus tell them, "My children, I will be with you only a little longer. You will look for me, and just as I told the Jews, so I tell you now: Where I am going, you cannot come" (John 13:33). After saying this, what could Jesus do to pick up the pieces of their shattered expectations and put them back together into a better picture of God's plan for their lives?

To begin with, Jesus explained where and why he was leaving. He said to them,

> "Do not let your hearts be troubled. You believe in God; believe also in me. My Father's house has many rooms; if that were not so, would I have told you that I am going there to prepare a place for you? And if I go and prepare a place for you, I will come back and take you to be with me that you also may be where I am" (John 14:1–3).

Rather than leave them alone, he intended for his departure to take their relationship to a whole new level. A body was prepared for Jesus so he could dwell with us while on earth. Now that his work was finished, he was preparing a place for his disciples to dwell with him in his Father's house. His physical absence was necessary to prepare for this glorious yet future transition.

He also consoled them by telling them that in his absence, they would benefit from the presence of God the Spirit, the third person of the Trinity. Jesus promised them, "I will ask the Father, and he will give you another advocate to help you and be with you forever—The Spirit of truth.... he lives with you and will be in you" (John 14:16–17).

Jesus's absence in their lives may have tempted them to feel abandoned and alone, set adrift in this world without any claim to God's family. But Jesus assured them that their feelings were unwarranted. He said, "I will not leave you as orphans; I will come to you" (John 14:18). Since both the Spirit and the Son are one and the same God, the coming of the Spirit is tantamount to the coming of the Son.

Jesus ended his upper room discourse with a prayer (see John chapter seventeen). In his prayer, he expressed the deepest desires of his heart. At the top of the prayer list was his longing for his disciples to be with him forever. He prayed, "Father, I want those you have given me to be with me where I am, and to see my glory, the glory you have given me because you loved me before the creation of the world" (John 17:24).

His prayer included a request that his disciples may enter a relationship with him that is akin to the relationship he enjoyed with his Father. Again, he prayed, "Father, just as you are in me and I am in you. May they also be in us so that the world may believe that you have sent me" (John 17:21).

The exciting thing about his prayer was that Jesus was not praying only for his immediate disciples. He was praying for us as well. Knowing the future and seeing the millions of people who would believe in him, Jesus said, "My prayer is not for them alone. I pray also for those who will believe in me through their message" (John 17:20).

We've been brought into the prayer circle of Jesus's love. His desire is for every one of us to enjoy the greatest presence of all: the gift of intimacy between God and humanity. To this I say with all my heart—Amen!

APPENDIX A

QUIZ ANSWERS

_J_ Most High – Mighty/Mighty One	A. Elohim
_H_ The Self-existent One	B. Adonai
_K_ Yahweh is My Banner	C. El Shaddai
_F_ Yahweh Who Heals	D. Yahweh Shalom
_I_ God	E. Soter
_A_ Mighty One – Majestic	F. Yahweh Rapha
_N_ Yahweh Our Righteousness	G. Alpha & Omega
_B_ Lord & Master	H. Yahweh
_E_ Savior	I. Theos/El
_C_ Almighty God/All-sufficient	J. El Elyon
_O_ Yahweh Will Provide	K. Yahweh Nissi
_D_ Yahweh is Peace	L. Yahweh Sabbaoth
_T_ Jesus – Yahweh is Savior	M. Christos
_M_ Messiah – The Anointed One	N. Yahweh Tsidkenu

THE GREATEST PRESENCE OF ALL

_L_ Yahweh of Hosts/Armies

_R_ The God Who Sees Me

_S_ The Everlasting God

_P_ The Lord Sanctifies, Makes Me Holy

_Q_ The Lord is Present

_G_ Beginning & The End

O. Yahweh Yireh

P. Yahweh M'Kaddesh

Q. Yahweh Shammah

R. El Roi

S. El Olam

T. Yeshua/Iesous

APPENDIX B

WHY YAHWEH?

MANY CONTEMPORARY BIBLE versions translate the name for God in Genesis 12:1 as "LORD." The original wording of this name, however, was most likely YHWH. These four Hebrew letters were written without vowel points. Sometime after the captivity, the Hebrew people substituted the name "Adonai" out of reverence for the personal name of God (see chapter three). This name means Lord or master. It is the meaning of the name "Adonal" that was carried on in early translations and versions, such as the Greek Septuagint (approximately 250 BC) and the Latin translation known as the Jerome Bible (approximately 400 AD).

Further changes to God's name were made over time. Hebrew scholars named Masoretes took the vowels from "Adonai" and inserted them between the consonants YHWH in a text they believed was faithful to the original Hebrew Bible (completed around the tenth century AD). At this point, YHWH was pronounced Yahweh. Scholars then changed the letter "Y" to a "J" to be read in the Latin vernacular. As a result, the name came to be pronounced as Jehovah.

The name Jehovah was used for almost a millennium until biblical scholars once again started referring to God here as Yahweh. I've chosen this version of the name to use throughout my book.

APPENDIX C
A WORD ON ANTINOMIES

THE BIBLE PRESENTS Jesus as both God and man. This is, however, hard to reconcile in our minds. How can the same person be both human and divine? In fact, there are other truths just as baffling: The Trinity, divine sovereignty, and human free will come to mind.

What we're describing are not logical contradictions, but antinomies. *Anti* means Against, and *nomos* means law. Sometimes God's revelation to man exceeds the level of human reasoning (see Isaiah 55:8–9) by stating as factual two things men cannot reconcile in their minds. Thus, antinomies wrestle with two equally valid principles. Unfortunately, we don't like to live in mental tension.

Wrong attempts have been made to resolve the God/man antinomy regarding the person of Christ. The first attempt is called Arianism. Arius (250–336 AD) was a church leader in Alexandria. He taught that Christ was the first and highest created being subordinate to God and of a different substance. The effect of his teaching was to deny the deity of Christ. The Council of Nicaea labeled his teachings as heretical in 325 AD.

Other attempts to resolve this antinomy involved denying the human nature of Christ (Gnosticism/Docetism and Apollinarianism), denying the one person of Christ (Nestorianism), and denying the two natures of Christ

(Monophysitism). Church councils from 325 to 451 AD debated and condemned all of these.

The biblical view is that Christ's natures are theanthropic: Christ has two natures, divine and human. These two natures are hypostatic: constituting one personal substance yet having two natures. The union of Christ's natures is constant: his two natures cannot be separated. A wrong calculus would be to view Christ as half God + half man = one person. This would render Christ a demigod akin to Achilles, Perseus, Hercules, and a host of other fictional characters in Greek and Roman mythologies. Instead, the right conclusion would be to view Christ as fully God + fully Man = one person. Thus, Jesus is the eternal God who also became man.

ACKNOWLEDGMENTS

I AM DEEPLY indebted to those who took the time to help me bring this book from the writer's pen to the reader's hands. My wife, daughter, and Suzanne supported me by providing insight into the style and content of the manuscript, arranging meetings with established authors, and making the purpose of the book come alive for the reader. I am grateful for Linda Nathan with Logos Word Designs who provided her many years of editing and writing experience to help make a rough draft ready for publication. In addition to correcting many grammatical blunders, she helped me to communicate ideas and concepts in a more personable way. I am also thankful for the administration, faculty, and staff at the school I have been privileged to teach at for the past thirty years. They graciously provided the fertile soil for my heart and mind to grow in grace and learn more about God's goodness. Above all, I am eternally grateful to our Savior who made Himself known to me and gave me the greatest message I could share with others—God's desire to be with us forever.

Jim Herring